Contents

Preface

Transport Economics is justifiably one of the most popular titles in the SEB series. Its author, Professor Colin Bamford, is not only an acknowledged expert in the field but also a Chief Examiner with a leading awarding body and a very clear communicator.

This edition retains the clarity and applied approach of the earlier editions but also adds more information on the significance of market structures and the current debate about the future of transport policy.

At a time when people are becoming increasingly interested in transport issues, OCR has launched a revised Transport Economics module for the new A level specification and more students are studying transport economics not only at A level but also at university level, this is a timely new edition.

Susan Grant
Series Editor

Introduction

The first edition of this book was published in 1995. In the relatively short space of time between then and the publication of this new third edition, transport issues have had a much higher profile from a popular and political perspective. Of particular relevance to the transport economist has been the publication of a major new policy statement ('A New Deal for Transport – Better for Everyone', DETR, 1998) followed by important new legislation to progress what is seen as a radical new approach to transport policy in the UK. The final chapter of this new edition analyses this policy and discusses its future implications.

Elsewhere:

- Chapter 5 has been substantially updated to include more material on the impact of deregulation and privatization on the local bus and rail markets respectively. This chapter now includes additional material on the economics of the market structures which can be applied to various transport markets.

- The statistics included in all chapters have been updated to 1999 wherever possible.

- New data response and structured essay questions are included. These are largely drawn from recent examination material produced by the three awarding bodies.

The approach throughout the text is to apply principles of economic analysis to a range of transport problems and issues, with a particular emphasis on micro-economics and market failure set within their macro-economic context. All chapters include reference to other books in the SEB series.

To keep up to date, students are strongly encouraged to read a quality newspaper – the transport issues featured in this book have an ever-increasing coverage in the national press. There is also an excellent website for the Department of the Environment, Transport and the Regions (www.detr.gov.uk) which now contains policy statements, consultation documents and statistical information. The more general Tutor2u site (www.tutor2u.co.uk) should also be consulted as this contains up-to-date short articles on current transport issues. The text includes some examples of indicative stimulus material that can be obtained from the above sources. In delivering their courses, teachers may well encourage students to build up a portfolio of similar items for use in the classroom.

The text is entirely compatible with the new AS/A2 Curriculum 2000 specifications of OCR, AQA and Edexcel. It is a recommended text for OCR's Module 2885 (Transport Economics) and will be of specific relevance to candidates taking AS Module 1 (AQA) and AS Unit 2 (Edexcel) as well as being of more general use at this level.

The book is also likely to be useful to UK students taking the examinations of the Institute of Logistics and Transport and for international students studying for the professional qualifications of the Chartered Institute of Transport. Undergraduates taking modules in this subject will also find the book of introductory value.

Since 1995 I have been encouraged by the feedback I have received from students and teachers. I have tried to take their comments into account in this new edition.

Chapter One

The nature of transport economics

'Transport is civilization.'   Rudyard Kipling

What is transport?

Transport is concerned with the movement of people and goods for a variety of personal and business purposes.

In studying transport movements, it is necessary to recognize two important but clearly interrelated elements, namely:

- the **infrastructure** – i.e. roads, railtrack, airspace and associated terminal facilities such as distribution centres, railway stations, ferry terminals and so on, on which movement takes place or on which transport needs are met
- the operation of transport vehicles – i.e. cars, lorries, trains, aircraft and vessels.

Making this distinction from the outset is important for the following reasons:

- Decisions on infrastructure are usually taken by the government directly (as is the case for roads), by the government indirectly (as was the case for railtrack and airports prior to privatization), or by privately owned transport businesses (e.g. distribution centres).
- Decisions on transport operations are in the main taken by private businesses, with little or no government involvement apart from there being an overall regulatory framework within which such operations can take place.

Consequently, there is a complex situation within transport. This can cause particular problems when students look at transport statistics and information.

Returning to the basic definition above, we can make the following observations:

- *Transport demand takes place over space and time.* All journeys are made over a particular distance, between start and end points, and take a particular amount of time. The reality, though, is that this demand is not spread evenly throughout the network, resulting in particular problems of congestion and, for many types of transport demand, some form of **peaking** whereby demand is concentrated at particular times of the day, week or year.

- Transport demand is a **derived demand** in the sense that it derives from the needs of people (to travel to work, to go shopping or to go on holiday) and the needs of businesses (to move goods and industrial materials). The function of transport, therefore, is to provide for the satisfaction of some other need.

These features are illustrated simply in Figure 1, which shows an adaptation of the circular flow of income.

The satisfaction of transport demand is met by various **transport modes,** such as roads, railways, aeroplanes, inland waterways and so on. Table 1 provides a brief analysis of the characteristics of the main modes that are used for carrying passengers and freight.

Although transport is used as a generic term throughout this book, an understanding of the modes and their characteristics is important. It particularly helps to explain the trends in transport demand that are

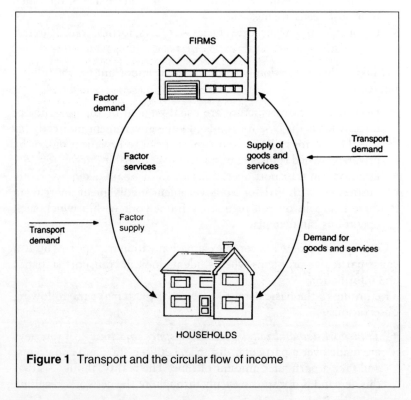

Figure 1 Transport and the circular flow of income

Table 1 Characteristics of the main modes of transport

Mode	Passengers	Freight
Rail	Potentially high speed over journeys of about 50–300 miles; can carry large volumes of passengers into city centres; environmentally acceptable	Bulk carrier, particularly over short distances; energy efficient; problems of interchange with road; likely to be more widely used in the future
Road	*Private car* is the most flexible and convenient of all transport modes; door to door service; comfortable and easily used for carriage of luggage, shopping etc.; *Buses* make the most efficient use of road space particularly in urban areas; main weaknesses relate to quality of service, reliability and comfort, relative to the car	Door to door service, highly used for 'just-in-time' deliveries; few transhipment problems, flexible, convenient and able to provide a high level of customer service; environmentally suspect and poor public image
Inland waterways	Some use for leisure and tourism purposes	Irrelevant in the UK but widely used for bulk carriage in other EU countries; relatively cheap but slow and inflexible compared with road and rail
Air	Speed is main strength, particularly over long distances; attractive for business and tourism; problem of intrinsic noise for those living on the flight paths	Very expensive; small carrying capacity but of obvious relevance where goods are of high value, perishable or urgent
Sea	Often the only possibility for certain types of trip; expensive on a mile for mile basis compared with other modes	Vast quantities can be moved; particular value for transport of containers over long distances
Pipelines		Well established for oil, bulk liquids, fuel and power; environmentally sound for inland use; a natural monopoly but subject to contestability

analysed in the next section, and many of the specific problems discussed in other chapters.

Transport demand in the UK

The demand for transport, of both passengers and goods, has been growing steadily over the past 50 years in the UK. Road transport is now the dominant mode in both the passenger and freight markets. There was a particular acceleration in total demand during the 1980s with a lesser rate of growth during the 1990s.

Figures 2 and 3 show the trend in the demand for transport in Great Britain from 1981 to 1999. The compound units used in each of these figures are indicative of the nature of transport; i.e. they measure demand in terms of both volume and distance for each of the main modes of passenger and goods transport.

More particularly, Figure 2 shows the following:

- Private cars were used for 85 per cent of all passenger transport demand in 1999.
- 93 per cent of demand is for road transport. Bus and coach transport, motor cycle and pedal cycle demand are added to that of transport by cars and vans to arrive at this figure.
- The use of rail remained relatively stable from 1981 to 1996 but since then there has been an 18 per cent increase in demand.
- The decline in use of buses and coaches has persisted, both absolutely and relatively over this period, but with stabilization since around 1993.

Correspondingly, Figure 3 shows the following:

- The total demand for goods transport has increased over the period, although recession from 1989 largely accounted for a fall in

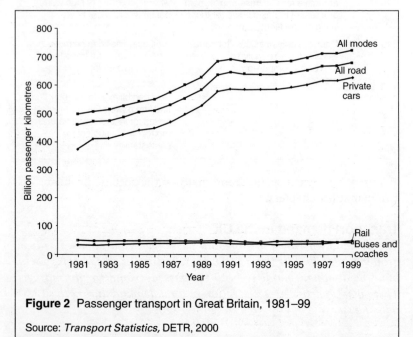

Figure 2 Passenger transport in Great Britain, 1981–99

Source: *Transport Statistics,* DETR, 2000

demand to 1992. By 1999, demand had grown by a further 15 per cent as the economy strengthened.

- Roads carried 65 per cent of all demand in 1999. If coastal shipping is excluded, roads had around 89 per cent of the inland market.
- The demand for transporting goods by rail fell over the early part of the period shown, but since 1994, there has been a 40 per cent increase in total demand. Future growth prospects are good.

Trends in transport demand since the mid-1980s are particularly relevant (see Table 2). They show a pronounced increase in the demand for road transport, for both passengers and goods. The implications of the trends shown in Figures 2 and 3 and in Table 2 are far-reaching for the future. Their recognition and understanding are important as they go some way to explaining the serious problems of traffic congestion being experienced on the UK's road network (see Chapter 6) and the need for a more sustainable future transport policy (see Chapter 7).

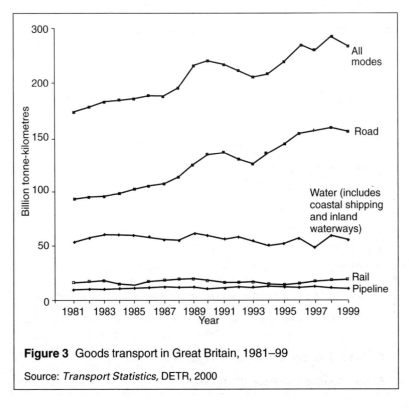

Figure 3 Goods transport in Great Britain, 1981–99

Source: *Transport Statistics,* DETR, 2000

Table 2 Transport trends in Great Britain since 1985

| | Passenger transport (billion passenger-km) | | | Goods transport (billion tonne-km) | |
	Cars and taxis	Buses and coaches	Rail	Road	Rail
1985	441	49	37	103.2	15.3
1986	465	47	37	105.4	16.6
1987	500	47	40	113.3	17.3
1988	536	46	41	130.2	18.2
1989	581	47	39	137.8	17.3
1990	588	46	40	136.3	15.8
1991	582	44	39	130.0	15.3
1992	583	43	38	126.5	15.5
1993	584	44	37	134.5	13.8
1994	591	44	35	143.7	13.0
1995	596	44	37	149.6	13.3
1996	606	44	39	153.9	15.1
1997	614	44	42	157.1	16.9
1998	617	45	44	159.5	17.4
1999	621	45	46	156.7	18.4

Source: *Transport Statistics,* DETR, 2000

Transport economics

The study of transport is now a recognized branch of economics. As the remainder of this book will show, many of the problems analysed and discussed by present-day transport economists can be seen as involving problems of **resource allocation**. Chapters 3–5 will consider some of these, including:

- how to allocate traffic, both passengers and goods, between the various transport modes, in particular between road and rail transport
- how to achieve the best allocation of public expenditure in transport
- how to achieve the right balance between the private and the public sectors, in infrastructure provision especially
- how best to meet the needs of users of transport while at the same time safeguarding the quality of the environment.

By looking at the functions of transport this introductory chapter has confirmed Rudyard Kipling's assertion that *transport is civilization*. Transport has an essential contribution to make to 'the industrial process' and to economic well-being in general. Through its ever-increasing use, the car is a need for most families, although whether this will be true to the same extent in the future is more problematic. The remaining chapters build upon this foundation and provide a more detailed perspective of the main resource allocation problems and issues in transport.

KEY WORDS

Infrastructure	Transport modes
Peaking	Resource allocation
Derived demand	

Further reading

Anderton, A., Unit 60 in *Economics*, 3rd edn, Causeway Press, 2000.

Grant, S., and Vidler, C., Unit 25 in *Economics in Context*, Heinemann, 2000.

Grant, S., Chapter 63 in Stanlake's *Introductory Economics*, 7th edn, Longman, 2000.

Sloman, J., Chapter 12 in *Economics*, 4th edn, Pearson Education, 2000.

Useful websites

Department of the Environment, Transport and the Regions: www.detr.gov.uk

Tutor2u: www.tutor2u.co.uk

Essay topic

(a) With examples, explain why transport is seen by economists as a 'derived demand'. [10 marks]

(b) The Department of Transport has estimated that the share of bus and coach traffic in the total market for travel in Great Britain will decline by up to 40 per cent over the next 25 years. Briefly explain how this estimate might have been made and comment upon its economic implications. [15 marks]

[OCR, March 1998]

Data response question

This task is from an OCR examination paper for November 1999. Read the data and then answer the questions that follow.

Motor vehicle traffic growth in the UK, 1965–2025

Over the past thirty-five years or so, there has been a consistent growth in motor vehicle traffic in the UK. Economists have put forward many reasons for this growth, one of which has been the growth in real GDP (see Figure A).

Traffic growth is forecast to persist over the next twenty-five years, as Figure B indicates. The implications of this growth for national transport policy are so serious that they cannot be ignored.

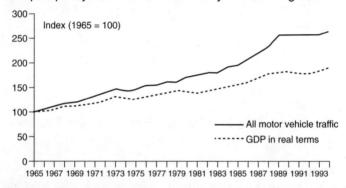

Figure A Motor vehicle traffic growth and Real Gross Domestic Product, 1965–1994

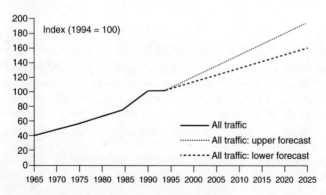

Figure B Motor vehicle traffic, 1965–2025

Source: Adapted from 'Developing an Integrated Transport Policy', Department of Environment, Transport and the Regions, 1997

1. With reference to Figure A,
   (a) Compare the growth of motor vehicle traffic and real GDP since 1965. [2 marks]
   (b) Excluding GDP, state and explain *two* other reasons for the growth in motor vehicle traffic since 1965. [4 marks]
2. With reference to Figure B,
   (a) Compare the forecast traffic growth from 1994 to 2025 with the actual traffic growth from 1965 to 1994. [2 marks]
   (b) What evidence is there to indicate that traffic forecasting is not likely to be exact? [2 marks]
   (c) How might a transport economist make use of these forecasts? [4 marks]
3. Explain the likely effects of the forecast increase in demand for motor vehicle transport on road and rail freight transport operators. [6 marks]

Chapter Two

The economic importance of transport

'*Transport links play an important role in the competitiveness of British business.*' Freight Transport Association, 1997

As Figures 2 and 3 indicated, the importance of transport activity can be shown crudely by the total demand for passenger and goods transport. In addition there are various other ways in which transport's economic importance can be analysed, including:

- employment in transport operations and related activities
- current and capital expenditure by consumers, households and the government.

Some of the statistics most widely used by economists are outlined in this chapter. Over the past few years, the range and quality of transport information has increased – students who wish to develop a wider awareness should consult *Transport Statistics – Great Britain* (Office of National Statistics, annual) and other government publications. Much of this information is also available on the DETR's website, www.detr.gov.uk.

Employment in transport

Transport is a substantial employer of labour in the UK economy. In 2000, for example, total transport employment was almost 1.9 million, or about one in twelve of the working population (see Table 3). About half of the total employment was in transport operations – that is, in the provision of road, rail, sea and air transport services for passengers and goods.

Over the last twenty to thirty years, total employment in transport operations has fallen, particularly in rail transport. This may seem surprising in view of the continued growth in demand, but it is a reflection of:

- the long-term decline of certain modes of transport – bus and sea transport especially
- the related switch from public to private passenger transport
- the massive job losses that have come about in rail transport, alongside substantial improvements in labour productivity

Table 3 Employment in transport, 1990–2000 (in thousands)

	1990	1995	2000
Transport operations			
Railways	138	113	49
Other inland transport (road freight, road passenger and urban railways)	379	357	451
Water transport	41	25	19
Air transport	56	54	85
Cargo handling and supporting services to transport	226	229	238
Travel agents and tour operators	69	75	103
Total	909	853	945
Employment in transport-related industries			
Motor vehicle production and parts	223	191	212
Other transport equipment	241	150	163
Retail distribution	316	324	381
Other	196	171	155
Total	976	837	911
All transport industries and services	1885	1690	1856

Source: Adapted from *Transport Statistics* (various)

- the increased efficiency of all modes of transport, through technological advances and improved transport vehicles and as a consequence of privatization.

Employment in **transport-related industries** is shown in the lower part of Table 3. Here, transport's economic importance as both a secondary and a tertiary activity is recognized. The decrease in employment in vehicle production was particularly severe – *it is a very good example of an industry whose fortunes have suffered as a consequence of deindustrialization.* Production has been transferred to countries with lower costs. The increase in employment since 1995 is largely accounted for by the further development of car assembly plants by Japanese manufacturers in the UK.

Expenditure on transport

Transport, like any form of economic activity, contributes to the national output of the UK economy. It is, though, a difficult task to estimate this contribution because transport is a part of the recorded output of many industries – retailing, construction, communications

Table 4 Index of road haulage activity and broad economic growth in Great Britain (1980 = 100)

Year	GDP	Manufacturing output	Construction output	Freight moved	Freight lifted	Average length of haul
1980	100	100	100	100	100	100
1985	111	102	111	110	104	106
1990	130	121	152	146	125	117
1991	127	114	140	139	114	122
1992	127	114	134	135	111	122
1993	129	115	133	143	116	124
1994	135	120	138	154	121	127
1995	138	123	137	160	122	131
1996	141	123	137	164	124	132
1997	144	125	141	167	124	133
1998	148	123	145	169	124	136
1999	152	123	145	166	119	139
Percentage change:						
1980–99	52	23	45	66	19	39
1994–99	13	3	5	8	–2	9

Source: *Economic Trends Table 2; Transport Statistics* (various)

and so on. Overall, transport accounts for around 15 per cent of GDP, which is slightly higher than in most other EU countries. In general, as national income has risen so too has the amount spent on transport. This expenditure is made by consumers and industry.

Table 4 and Figure 4 show that since the mid-1980s, the rate of increase of demand for road freight transport has increased at a faster rate than the growth of GDP. In contrast, the rate of growth in manufacturing output has been consistently below that of GDP growth (indicative of deindustrialization), and in recent years the rate of growth of output from construction has lagged behind that of road freight transport. It is also interesting to note that the average length of haul has increased steadily and consistently since 1980.

Table 5 shows weekly household expenditure on transport and travel from 1987 to 1999. Over much of this period, as a percentage of *all* **household expenditure**, the amount spent on transport and travel remained more or less steady at around 15 per cent increasing to 17 per cent in 1999. Within this, though, the absolute amount and proportion of total expenditure spent on the purchase and running of private cars has increased very rapidly. This is in line with the trends identified in Figure 2.

It is also interesting to observe that there has been an increase in

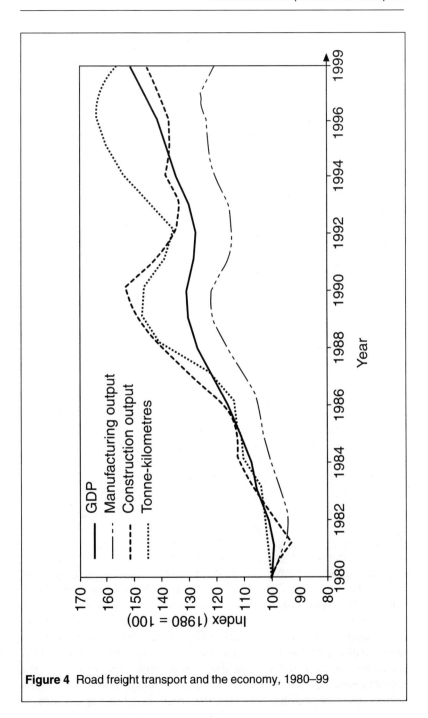

Figure 4 Road freight transport and the economy, 1980–99

Table 5 Household expenditure on transport and travel, 1987–99 (£ per week)

	1987	1991	1996	1999
Net purchase of motor vehicles	11.68	17.08	15.25	23.70
Maintenance and running of motor vehicles	12.12	17.04	21.74	28.10
Railway and tube fares	0.89	0.96	1.28	1.90
Bus and coach fares	1.14	1.25	1.25	1.30
Other	2.57	3.37	3.64	3.70
All transport and travel	28.40	39.70	43.16	58.7
Motoring expenditure as % of total	83.8	85.9	85.7	86.3
Percentage of household expenditure	15.1	15.3	14.9	17.0

Source: Adapted from *Family Expenditure Survey,* ONS, 1999

household expenditure in real terms of over 20 per cent for the period covered by Table 5. The *Family Expenditure Survey* also shows two further interesting points:

- The percentage of household expenditure spent on transport and travel increases as household income increases. *There is a high, positive income elasticity of demand,* so sales expand when incomes are increasing. Conversely – as shown by declining car sales and fewer foreign holidays being bought – when the economy moves into recession then sales tend to decline.
- Railways and private cars are used primarily by households in the higher income groups; in contrast, bus transport is used disproportionately by the lower income groups. *The demand for bus travel therefore has a low income elasticity of demand* – whether it is an inferior good is not an easy question to answer because it depends on complex factors relating to an individual's travel needs.

Transport is an important part of **public expenditure**, the total money spent by central and local governments on the provision of various goods and services in the UK.

Annually, transport expenditure accounts for 7–8 per cent of the total. This money is expended by central and local governments on both **capital** and **current expenditure**. The former covers major items of transport expenditure spread over various years, for example the construction of a new by-pass, whereas the latter relates to items such as annual maintenance costs and **revenue support** (fares subsidies). The largest sums go

Table 6 Expenditure on transport subsidies and grants, 1987–99 (£ million)

	1987	1991	1996	1999
Rail:				
National support	946	1168	1874	1111
London Transport:				
Core business	343	702	938	816
Bus and local rail services:				
Revenue support	229	235	447	600
Concessionary fares	371	440	427	

Source: Adapted from *Transport Statistics* (various)

into the national and local road systems (see also Chapter 4).

It is interesting to see from Table 6 that, for transport in London and by rail, grants and subsidies paid have increased in recent years, contrary to popular belief. Significantly, that paid to support local bus services outside London has fallen.

Equally pertinent has been the continued expenditure on the **Public Service Obligation** paid to the railways. This money is the government's contract with train operators to safeguard certain unremunerative passenger services outside the metropolitan areas, where the Passenger Transport Executives (PTEs) have this particular responsibility. In 1996, this sum was inflated by payments made to the new private franchised train operating companies but, since then, it has fallen on an annual basis (see Chapter 5).

As J. M. Thomson once stated, transport 'requires capital equipment, materials and labour'. Moreover, it is an important source of private and public sector expenditure on both infrastructure and transport operations. Transport growth is therefore inextricably linked to personal and business well-being and has an important role in the competitiveness of British business.

KEY WORDS

Transport-related industries	Capital expenditure
	Current expenditure
Household expenditure	Revenue support
Public expenditure	Public Service Obligation

Further reading
Anderton, A., Unit 60 in *Economics*, 3rd edn, Causeway Press, 2000.
Beardshaw, J., *et al.*, Chapter 28 in *Economics: A Student's Guide*, 4th edn, Longman, 1998.
Grant, S., and Vidler, C., Unit 25 in *Economics in Context*, Heinemann, 2000.
Griffiths, A., and Wall, S., Chapter 12 in *Applied Economics*, 8th edn, Longman, 2000.

Useful websites
Biz/ed: www.bizded.ac.uk
National Statistics: www.statistics.gov.uk/statbase.mainmenu.asp

Essay topic
Explain the criteria that an economist would use to analyse the importance of transport in the UK economy.   [25 marks]

Data response question

Passenger transport in the UK
This task is based on a specimen question produced by Edexcel for the new AS/A level examinations from 2001. Study Figures A–D relating to transport, and then answer the questions that follow.

Figure A

Source: *The Independent,* 26 July 1994

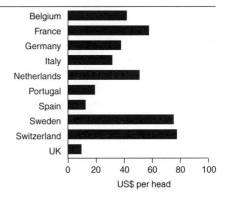

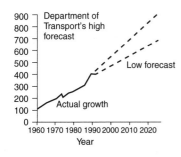

Figure B UK road traffic growth (billion vehicle-km per year)

Source: *The Independent,* 27 October 1994

Figure C UK passenger transport (billion passenger-km per year)

Source: *The Independent,* 27 October 1994

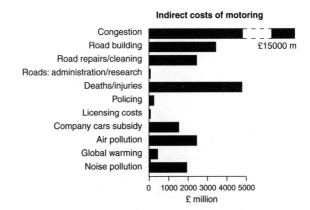

Indirect costs of motoring

Congestion £15000 m
Road building
Road repairs/cleaning
Roads: administration/research
Deaths/injuries
Policing
Licensing costs
Company cars subsidy
Air pollution
Global warming
Noise pollution

0 1000 2000 3000 4000 5000
£ million

Revenue from road users

Figure D UK road transport costs and revenue, 1993

Source: *The Independent,*
26 July 1994

Fuel tax
Vehicle excise duty £10700 m

0 1000 2000 3000 4000 5000
£ million

1. (a) With reference to the data, how might the changing pattern of transport use in the UK be explained? [8 marks]
   (b) What other information would you find useful in explaining these changes? [4 marks]
2. (a) With reference to Figure D, how does the use of private cars give rise to external costs? [4 marks]
   (b) To what extent do the taxes levied on road users compensate for the external costs of motoring? [3 marks]
3. Examine *one* policy which might be used to reduce the growth of road traffic in the next 20 years. [6 marks]

Chapter Three

Transport costs and pricing

'The private car liberates but it also destroys ... We are nourishing at immense cost a monster of great potential destructiveness ... and yet we love him dearly!' Sir Colin Buchanan, 1963

The nature of transport costs

Economists recognize three types of costs, which have particular relevance to transport. These are:

- **Private costs** – the opportunity costs to the individual or firm of resources used. These are based on the market value of factors purchased and include the direct operating cost paid in running various types of transport vehicle.
- **External costs** – the spillover effects which can occur if private costs and social costs are not equal. A feature of most transport operations is that these costs do occur and are *negative*.
- **Social costs** – the opportunity costs to the whole of society of the resources an individual or firm uses. In other words, these are the total costs of transport use – private plus external costs.

Figure 5 illustrates the idea that if market demand and supply correctly reflect the marginal benefit of consumption and the marginal cost of production of a good, then there will be an efficient allocation of resources at P_o and Q_o. Here, the price at which the goods are sold equals the marginal cost of producing them; that is $P = MC$. The marginal social cost (MSC) of providing a commodity or service equals the marginal social benefit (MSB) derived from its consumption.

This optimum does not occur in most transport markets, where the private costs and benefits fail to reflect adequately the costs and benefits to society of providing the services concerned. External costs in the form of traffic congestion, noise pollution, exhaust emissions and so on do occur, with marginal social cost greater than marginal private cost. Consequently, *there is a misallocation of resources* as the MSB and MSC curves differ from the market demand and supply curves. Moreover, there is a powerful case for government intervention in such markets to improve the allocation of resources (see below).

Private costs, as shown in Table 7, can be subdivided into three main elements, namely:

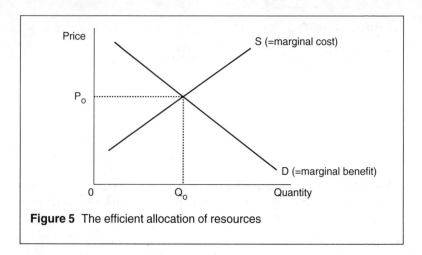

Figure 5 The efficient allocation of resources

Table 7 Cost structure of main modes of transport operations

Mode	Fixed costs	Variable costs	Other
Private cars	Capital costs, insurance, road tax, depreciation	Fuel, maintenance, tyres	–
Heavy goods vehicles	Capital costs, licences, insurance, depreciation	Fuel, maintenance, tyres, drivers' wages	Depot costs
Rail	Track costs, capital costs, administrative and overhead charges	Fuel, maintenance, labour costs	Interchange costs
Air	Capital costs, administrative and overhead charges	Fuel, maintenance, landing charges, in-flight services, labour costs	
Sea	Capital costs, insurance, administrative and overhead charges	Fuel, maintenance, in-voyage costs, harbour costs	

- **Fixed costs** – these in general consist of the costs of making transport vehicles available for use. Rail is unusual in so far as track costs have to be included.
- **Variable costs** – these directly depend on the way in which transport vehicles are used and the level of service that is available.
- Other costs – in most cases these can be included in fixed costs and cover the costs of depots, distribution centres and rail interchanges.

This distinction is important. In railway operation, for example, fixed costs are a relatively high proportion of total costs. Once a stretch of railway track is open for use, the average cost per train falls as the number of trains using the line increases.

Table 8 shows a cost breakdown in these terms for three sizes of heavy goods vehicle. It introduces a further cost concept, that of **semi-fixed costs** – that is, costs that are not entirely dependent on the use made of vehicles. In this case, firms normally have a core staff of drivers to pay, even though they may not always be fully employed in working with the vehicles. This table also illustrates how firms can benefit from **economies of scale** – a reduction in long-run average costs – through the use of heavier goods vehicles. The average cost per tonne of payload of 38-tonne vehicle operation is 7.6 per cent less than that of operating 32.5-tonne vehicles, the legal permitted maximum until May 1983. This particular benefit is a very powerful one which has been used by industry to support their argument for 44-tonne operations.

An additional benefit of larger vehicles is that fewer vehicles would be needed to move a given tonnage of goods. In turn, this would mean fewer vehicles on the roads, reduced congestion, fuel savings and certain environmental benefits. The downside, though, is that it would make it more difficult for the railways to gain new freight business.

Table 8 Annual costs of operating three types of large goods vehicle*

	32.5-tonnes (£)	38 tonnes (£)	44 tonnes (£)
Fixed costs			
Overhead costs	10514	11539	12600
Depreciation	8618	11596	3022
Licences/insurance	6710	7159	6240
Semi-fixed costs			
Drivers' wages	12509	13135	13634
Variable costs			
Fuel/oil	15030	17502	20280
Tyres	3024	3354	3870
Maintenance	6504	6696	7200
Total operating costs	**62909**	**70981**	**66846**
Typical payload	20 tonnes	24.5 tonnes	29.5 tonnes
Cost per tonne of payload	3145	2897	2266

*Based on 100000 km per annum

Source: Motor Transport Cost Tables, 1995

Recognizing these conflicts, the government announced that from January 1999 the maximum permitted weight of goods vehicle would be increased to 41 tonnes, for five-axle combinations. The 44-tonne maximum applied only where vehicles are carrying containers and swap-bodies to and from rail terminals. Whether to increase the maximum weight of goods vehicle above 41 tonnes has proved to be a controversial issue. The matter was referred to the Commission for Integrated Transport (CFIT) which, after much deliberation, recommended that 44-tonne vehicles with six axles could use our roads from February 2001. This weight increase has put us in line with other EU countries and should result in:

- fewer vehicles on the road – 6500–9000 estimated
- a further modest reduction in distribution costs (approximately 10 per cent less per tonne of payload)
- less wear and tear on road surfaces, and cleaner engines, emitting less damaging pollutants.

A key issue in the debate has been whether 44-tonne vehicles would adversely affect the volume of freight traffic on the railways. After careful study, the CFIT thought not; it also chose to ignore the environmental costs, much to the concern of pressure groups such as Friends of the Earth (see extract).

Monster truck invasion

Monster juggernauts could soon be thundering through Britain's towns and villages amid huge safety and environmental protests. Plans to raise the weight limit of lorries to 44 tonnes will be published tomorrow, amidst fears that this could increase to an alarming 60 tonnes if Europe has its way.

Roger Higman, of Friends of the Earth, warned last night that any increases would have a catastrophic effect. He said: 'Heavy lorries kill lots of people. They are responsible for a considerable amount of pollution. They damage roads and bridges, costing the taxpayer millions in repairs.'

He added that 'People have been told again and again that bigger lorries mean fewer lorries. But we have just ended up with more and more traffic. The Government's priority should be getting heavy lorries off the roads and more freight on to trains. The argument about axles is irrelevant. It's the weight of the truck that causes the damage.'

Shadow Foreign Secretary Francis Maude said: 'The last thing the British people want is juggernauts roaring through quiet towns and villages.'

Adapted from the *Sunday Express,* 21 March 2000

A further application of these cost concepts is in passenger transport, where 'load factors' are an important consideration. This term refers to the proportion of space or seats offered for sale which is actually paid for and taken up by fare-paying passengers. Perhaps the best illustration is in air transport where fixed costs are a high proportion of total costs. Because of this, very lucrative last-minute deals are often provided by tour operators for people looking for a cheap holiday! Variable costs have to be covered but the price paid is also likely to make a contribution to fixed costs.

The external costs of transport

Transport, of course, contributes to the environmental problems that face us. There is little argument that transport pollutes the environment and, through CO_2 emissions, it is a major contributor to the greenhouse effect and global warming. Within transport it is the road sector that attracts most criticism and cause for concern. Other modes, particularly rail, are more environmentally friendly for the carriage of passengers and freight than road transport.

At a more local level, transport imposes much more localized external costs, particularly on those living and working in urban areas close to main roads, transport depots and so on. These **negative externalities** include:

- *Noise pollution.* Lorries in particular cause high levels of disturbance. Traffic noise produces a level of pitch which over long periods becomes unwelcome to the human ear. Prolonged exposure to traffic noise can disrupt lifestyle, increase stress and make it difficult to relax.
- *Atmospheric pollution.* Road traffic produces CO_2 emissions, particularly from exhaust systems. As with noise, the local incidence of pollution from lorries is greater than that from cars. Diesel engines are rather 'greener' than their petrol equivalents, although there is particular concern over nitrous oxide emissions.
- *Visual intrusion.* This is a less obvious negative externality and relates to situations where road traffic impairs or devalues the view in an urban or rural landscape. Sadly, in many historic cities, buildings seem to rise from a plinth of cars and visitors and residents obtain less visual enjoyment than they might from their surroundings.
- *Blight.* Again, urban road transport is the main culprit. This type of negative externality is invariably caused by planning and similar problems associated with the building of new roads or providing

'Smash the next lamp on the left, flatten the pavement by the pub, nudge the sweetshop, scrape the Market Cross, then just follow the skidmarks to London.'

Widower's nightmare

SUZANNA CHAMBERS

A father whose wife was killed when a runaway lorry careered through a town attacked plans to allow bigger juggernauts on to Britain's roads.

Glenn Rooke, 47, said last night that he was horrified to learn the Government was proposing to raise the weight limits for lorries from 40 to 44 tonnes.

His wife, Angela, was one of six people killed when a 22-tonne truck smashed into a newspaper shop and two houses in the West Yorkshire town of Sowerby Bridge in 1993.

Mr Rooke, who now lives in Halifax, said: 'You just can't have something like a 44-tonne lorry driving through a small village. They have to be restricted to motorways where they are less of a hazard.' He said juggernauts of that size would take a lot longer to slow down, making them more dangerous. An investigation following the accident, which left father Peter Stott and mother Beryl Rose among the dead, found that all the brakes of the lorry were worn out.

Mr Rooke – who has three children, a 14-year-old and 11-year-old twins – said he would worry more about them walking along the road if the larger juggernauts were allowed.

Dr Paul Thomas, who campaigned for more than 10 years to ban heavy goods vehicles from his picturesque village of Tingewick, Bucks, said: 'I dread to think what would happen if lorries that size came through.'

Source: *Sunday Express,* 21 March 2000

facilities to speed up the traffic flow.
- *Community severence and damage from vehicles* (see cartoon).
- *Accidents.* Road traffic accidents are very costly to the community, in terms of the physical damage caused and in the serious injuries and loss of life which can occur (see box above).

The above are in addition to further negative externalities as a consequence of traffic congestion (see Chapter 6).

These problems were recognized by the Royal Commission on Environmental Pollution (RCEP) in 1971 when it produced its first report. In 1994 and in 1997, the Commission has published highly critical and controversial reports, in which it has proposed a fundamental shift and complete rethink on transport policy. Details of their proposals are contained in Chapter 7. The boxed item below shows their estimates for these negative externalities.

Underlying the recommendations is the fact that, at present, owing to negative externalities, the price paid by the transport users is lower and the quantity demanded is greater than the **social optimum** at which price equals marginal social cost. This situation is shown in Figure 6. As things stand, there is no incentive to reduce transport demand as users do not pay the full or true cost involved. Moreover, vehicle users gain at the expense of other groups in society. The economist's answer here is to introduce an **indirect tax** (or 'green tax') to equate marginal social cost and marginal social benefit. (See also Figure 15.)

The estimated external and social costs of road transport in Great Britain (£ billion a year, 1994 prices)

Air pollution	2.0–5.2
Climatic change	1.5–3.1
Noise and vibration	1.0–4.6
Total external costs	4.5–12.9
Road accidents	5.4
Social costs of road transport	9.9–18.3

Note: The estimates of external costs are very difficult to measure with precision, hence the range of values shown. They do, though, provide a broad indication of the scale of harm caused by road transport. The costs of congestion are not included.

This approach is fine in theory, but in practice it is very difficult to apply, not least because there are genuine obstacles to recognizing and measuring all the social costs and benefits involved. Even so, the RCEP do clearly acknowledge that negative externalities are a serious issue and that a radical sea-change approach is needed in order to avert ever-more serious environmental problems from increased transport demand.

The track costs argument

Over the past twenty years or so, economists have debated the 'track costs' argument, particularly in the context of road provision. In short, it involves the issue of who pays and who benefits from the way in which roads are provided.

Table 9 shows the basis of this argument. The final column indicates that all classes of users in 1994/95 covered their track costs; that is, the construction and maintenance costs allocated to them for the use that they made of the road network. As the table shows, cars especially cover track costs by a magnitude of 3.7 to 1. This has increased since 1994, although no reliable estimates are available. Heavy goods vehicles and buses and coaches also cover their direct road costs but by the smallest proportion of any class of user, 1.4:1. The total tax paid by road users consists of various indirect taxes such as fuel tax, car tax, vehicle excise duty, value added tax and so on.

The original idea behind the Road Fund Tax (the Vehicle Excise Duty as it is now known) was that receipts from it were to be ploughed back into the road network to provide for users. In other words, it was **hypothecated** for road-building and on-going maintenance. This is no longer the case. On the contrary, there are valid arguments, related to the cost of externalities, why private car users should pay additional taxation. Commercial vehicles, because of their production-related use of roads, should similarly only be taxed to cover their direct road costs. The information in Table 9 can therefore be used to argue for:

- less taxes to be paid by commercial vehicle users and buses and coaches
- even higher taxes for private car users.

This view, indeed, is one that has been promoted for some time by the Freight Transport Association, the leading user trade association in freight transport in the UK. The boxed item on the previous page shows a summary of their 'Transport Dilemma' arguments. The data

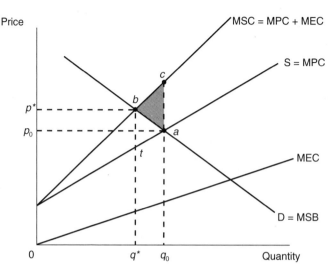

(MEC = marginal external costs; MPC = marginal private costs; MSC = marginal social costs)

Allocative efficiency is achieved where MSC = MSB.

The MSC schedule is the vertical sum of MPC and MEC.
The private market extends production to q_0, where D = S,
but for each unit between q^* and q_0, MSC is greater than MSB.
These units should not be produced.
The deadweight loss from their production is given by the shaded
triangle *abc*.

Consequently:

Social costs	>	Private costs
[Total costs of use of road space]		[Costs of use of road space to users]

Quantity demanded is higher than optimum.
Price paid by users is lower than optimum.

REMEDY: INCREASED TAXATION SO THAT MSC = MSB
(a green tax)

Figure 6 Private and social costs divergence

The slow road to hypocrisy

LORD HANSON

To own a car has been a lifelong dream for most of us and an unmatched blessing. Its speed, reliability and ready availability, undreamed of in the past, give us a mobility and freedom now taken for granted.

The car supports the breadwinner's job and improves family life and leisure in ways that not even the most comprehensive system of public transport could ever provide. But this great personal boon is now under threat.

Many a motorist will be asking if there is no one in the public arena prepared to speak up for the car, or in favour of building new roads. Do our lives have to be governed by "green" minorities? Is no one willing to admit doubts over the so-called merits of a Whitehall-inspired "integrated" public system?

Instead the embattled car owner is offered one daft scheme after another. The latest suggestion is to curb the use of the M5 and M6 motorways by restricting access for local drivers.

The recent government about-face on roads neatly encapsulates our double standards. The Chancellor of the Exchequer puts a swingeing increase on the existing 72 per cent tax on petrol and diesel, despite the fact that less than 30 per cent of the £23 billion taxes raised on motoring is used for road building and maintenance. It seems that motorists are being used as a milch-cow for all those other areas that the State wants to spend our money on.

John Prescott, the minister responsible, supposedly a great friend of the working – and driving – man, adds his bit with the review or cancellation of vitally-needed road improvements. In what century are these people that dream up our transport policy living?

When Prescott had to make a decision on 12 contentious road schemes, he stopped two, approved five and deferred decisions on five... Why the indecision when the argument for new roads is compelling?

Despite the cost – easily affordable from the road fund tax – better roads are essential to reduce the gridlocks that bedevil us. And we must encourage ample parking in towns. North America can give us lessons because new businesses will only open if they can be sure their customers can get to them...

When we consider road freight, in which business I spent most of my early working days, the prospect is frightening. Ninety per cent of goods go by road. No imaginable future or past railway system could, with such ease, flexibility and cheapness, bring us the fresh food and other products we need daily.

Who of us is prepared to pay for the cost and inconvenience of having essential goods delayed by rail? Not the merchants, certainly, nor especially the consumer and tax-paying voter.

Cars and lorries – the latter pay the bulk of the road and fuel taxes – are blamed for pollution, but this ignores the massive technological advances in engine design that have reduced emissions by 90 per cent in the past 20 years and will continue to make motoring even cleaner...

Of course, as car critics like to point out, there are still too many road injuries. But the number of fatalities has halved since 1966. Let us not forget that statistics show the home is a most dangerous place, yet no one suggests its abolition.

The roads solution is to find a balance between safety and some discomfort on the one hand and personal freedom of choice on the other. All the evidence is that current planned road improvements are vital to move us into the next century. They are also vital for the economic growth of the country, not forgetting the car industry and the road materials companies which will survive or fail on this.

Source: *Express on Sunday*, 17 August 1997

Table 9 Projected road taxation and track costs

Class of vehicle	Total tax	Road costs	Taxes:cost ratio
Cars, light vans and taxis	14 610	3 990	3.7:1
Motorcycles	70	20	3.5:1
Buses and coaches	360	255	1.4:1
Goods vehicles below 3.5 tonnes gvw	2 740	2 030	1.4:1
Other vehicles	320	155	2.1:1
Totals	**18 100**	**6 450**	

Source: Adapted from *Transport Statistics,* Department of Transport, 1994

response question at the end of this chapter puts an alternative point of view.

Notwithstanding this, looking ahead, future taxation policy is most likely to continue the trend of increasing the level of taxation on private road users as this goes some way to meeting the very strong environmental arguments raised in the previous section for cutting back on private car use and using vehicles much more efficiently than at present.

THE TRANSPORT DILEMMA

The Freight Transport Association believes that the demand for freight transport will continue to increase over the next 20 years, probably above government forecasts. At the same time, congestion will get worse.

All road users must share the responsibility for making best use of transport resources. There must be an on-going commitment to a package of measures leading to the maximum investment in transport infrastructure. Cars are and always will be the main problem – the whole population must make a determined effort to curb the use of cars and promote a greater use of and commitment to public transport. This will allow road freight vehicles to move around more efficiently.

The ultimate aim must be one of hypothecation of infrastructure funds from road user revenues. There must be an irrevocable commitment to a new roads programme and a minimum standard created for access to ports, cities, industrial and urban areas.

Source: Adapted from *Transport Dilemma: Caring for Society's Freight Transport Needs Over the Next 20 Years,* Freight Transport Association, 1991

Price discrimination

Within a broadly defined market, different market segments are likely to have different price elasticities of demand. In such circumstances, the theory behind **price discrimination** is that *total revenue will be maximized if marginal revenues are equalized across all market segments,* in order to determine the quantities to be offered in each segment. Prices are then set in accordance with the price elasticity of demand in each segment. The more inelastic the demand, the higher the price. In the extreme cases, each customer would be treated individually and be charged a price which reduced his or her **consumer surplus** to zero and thus maximized total revenue for the producer.

In practice, perfect price discrimination as described above is not possible. Appropriate market segments therefore need to be price identified, and estimates made of the price elasticity of demand in each case. Pricing systems must be developed, which not only raise prices in the less elastic market segments, but also prevent those customers from trading down to the cheaper segments.

The UK rail passenger market has experienced this form of pricing since the early 1970s, particularly for longer distance and intercity tickets. On routes to London the business travel segment is particularly significant, and competition from other modes, including the private car, is relatively weak. *Price elasticities are estimated at less than unity,* particularly for arrival in London in time for morning business meetings. Thus tickets for such journeys command the highest prices.

In the leisure and social travel markets, including visiting friends and relatives, competition from other modes such as express coaches is stronger, and the precise time of travel is less important. *Price elasticities of demand in these market segments are greater than unity.* Much lower fares are offered to extract revenue through increased volumes of business in these segments, but availability of these cheaper tickets is restricted to minimize their use by business travellers.

In the market segments most sensitive to price (where competition from other modes is strongest and where customers may be less well off and are likely to be disuaded from travel altogether), further discounts are given. These are frequently given via railcards such as the Family Railcard, the Senior Railcard and the Young Persons Railcard, because once again these schemes promote increased volumes of traffic but minimize the loss of revenue from segments such as business travel where price elasticities are significantly lower.

Price differentials between market segments are often substantial because of the significant variations in demand elasticities. This point

Table 10 Standard Class rail fares between Leeds and King's Cross (London), November 2000

Open Return	£114	This ticket is aimed at the business travel market and is completely unrestricted
Saver Return	£64	This fare offers a huge reduction on the Open Return but cannot be used for arrival in London before 11.30 a.m.
Day Return	£23	Available for most off-peak journeys. Advance booking is required
Great Value Return	£36	As above but valid for one month
Fab 4	£54	Cheapest fare per head. Allows up to 4 people travelling together on one ticket. Advance booking is required

is clearly shown in Table 10, which demonstates the wide range of fares available for rail travellers between Leeds and London.

Transport subsidy and its effects on pricing

On many passenger transport services, there is little prospect that fares can be set at levels which will generate large volumes of business and provide a commercial rate of return to the operator. Many urban, suburban and rural bus and rail services fall into this category. (See also Chapter 5.)

In principle, the availability of **subsidies** or revenue support can help to reduce the prices paid by passengers, and to boost patronage on the services concerned. This will generate a range of social benefits such as reduced traffic congestion and enhanced mobility for the less well off.

As shown by Figure 7, the receipt of subsidy by transport operators acts to shift the supply curve down and to the right, so that any selected output can be offered to the public at a reduced price. Intersection with the downward-sloping demand curve re-establishes market equilibrium with the quantity increased to Q_2 and the price reduced to P_2.

In practice, however, the use of subsidies to fund fare reductions is not widespread in the UK and has been decreasing in real terms. Subsidies to bus operators to maintain fares at low levels are relatively uncommon outside larger urban areas. Many rural local authorities provide subsidies only to pay for fare reductions to identified groups in need, such as pensioners and the disabled. Subsidies on unprofitable rural rail routes simply cover the notional shortfall in the costs of operating such routes, and

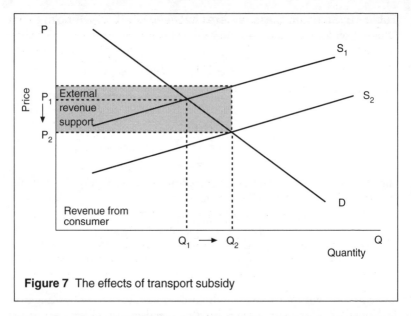

Figure 7 The effects of transport subsidy

fares reflect the national level of rail fares rather than the level of subsidy received.

It is in the main conurbations, and particularly the metropolitan areas, *where local subsidies for bus and rail services are reflected in the prices charged to the general traveller.* In some regions the fares reduction due to the level of subsidy can be quite significant.

In England, the following trends in central and local government expenditure on transport subsidies can be identified since 1991/92:

- Expenditure on concessionary fares for senior citizens and young people has been relatively stable over the last three years at around £450 million.
- Revenue support for local bus services fell until 1997/98 when it was £227 million. It rose to £270 million in 1998/99.
- Revenue support for rail services in metropolitan areas outside London has increased significantly, owing to the continued committment by Passenger Transport Executives to local rail network development. In 1999/2000 this stood at £230 million, a one-third increase on 1996/97.
- All subsidies and grants for transport in London have increased to £816 million in 1999/2000, a one-third increase on 1997/98.

The main argument for subsidizing passenger transport, therefore, is one of **social equity**. Transport is provided at a subsidized fare and, in some cases, certain groups in the community who cannot afford to pay the full market price receive particular benefit or support for cheaper travel. There are other arguments to support subsidies being paid to passenger transport. These include the following:

- *Where public transport, such as in large towns and cities, generates* **positive externalities.** Urban bus and rail services, for example, make a much better use of roadspace than private cars, and an efficient passenger transport system can help to reduce the effects of traffic congestion.
- *Where new transport facilities may help in* **urban regeneration,** *such as in the case of new rapid transit systems like the Manchester Metrolink and Sheffield Supertram projects.* In such cases, a new Light Rail Transit system may help to attract new businesses and create jobs to previously run-down parts of the city.
- *Where it is desirable to encourage the use of public transport for environmental reasons,* such as with a park and ride system in an historic city such as Cambridge or York or in congested cities like Nottingham and Leicester.

Not all economists agree with these arguments. There are other views as to why the level of subsidy should be reduced. These include:

- The blanket nature of subsidy means that it is difficult to direct subsidy to those who really need it. Perhaps the best example of this is rail commuter fares, where all travellers, regardless of income, pay the same fare.

- The view that subsidy breeds inefficiency. It is invariably the case that the costs of public sector transport operators are higher than those in the private sector; consequently operating costs are higher than they need be.

- The idea that managers of subsidized businesses lack motivation to keep costs down, and so reduce the drain on the public purse.

These latter arguments have had a significant bearing on transport policy towards local bus services and the railways (see Chapter 5). The government is not against subsidy as such – what it does require, though, is that, where a subsidy is paid, then the receipt of public money should make its recipients more accountable.

In retrospect, much of what Sir Colin Buchanan had to say about the problems of traffic in towns has been shown to be correct. It is a matter of some regret that a generation of transport planners, who have seemingly been implementing his ideas, have not paid more attention to the man who saw it all coming. For Lord Hanson, though, the preservation of the personal freedom which only the car can provide is an overriding consideration.

KEY WORDS

Private costs	Indirect tax
External costs	Track costs
Social costs	Allocative efficiency
Fixed costs	Hypothecated
Variable costs	Price discrimination
Semi-fixed costs	Consumer surplus
Economies of scale	Subsidies
Load factors	Social equity
Negative externalities	Positive externalities
Social optimum	Urban regeneration

Further reading

Beardshaw, J., *et al.*, Chapter 28 in *Economics: A Student's Guide*, 4th edn, Longman, 2000.

Burningham, D., and Davies, J., Chapters 2 and 3 in *Green Economics*, 2nd edn. Heinemann, 1999.

Griffiths, A., and Wall, S., Chapter 10 in *Applied Economics*, 8th edn, Longman, 1999.

Munday, S., Chapter 4 in *Markets and Market Failure*, Heinemann, 2000.

Useful websites

EU transport: www.europa.eu.int/en/comm/dg07/index.htm
Government Environment Agency: www.environment-agency.gov.uk

Essay topics

1. In September 1997, the city authorities in Paris experimented with a one-day ban on all vehicles with even registration plates in order to improve air quality, which had deteriorated to a damaging level.

    (a) How do economists represent the externalities involved in the above situation? [8 marks]

(b) Discuss what other measures the authorities could plan to introduce in order to improve traffic and environmental conditions in the city in the longer term. [12 marks]
[OCR, November 1999]

2. (a) Explain the difference between subsidy and cross-subsidization. [8 marks]

(b) Discuss why under certain circumstances economists might regard subsidy as efficient and cross-subsidization as inefficient. [12 marks]

Data response question

This task is from an OCR examination paper in March 2000. Read the newspaper extract and study the data on freight transport, then answer the questions that follow.

Rail freight gathering steam

'After many years of steady and consistent decline, the newly privatized operator of rail freight services in the UK, English, Welsh and Scottish Railways (EWS), has experienced an unprecedented boom in its business in the last year. Major retailers such as Sainsbury's, Safeway and Superdrug have started to use rail freight rather than road for some of their primary long-haul distribution; large companies such as Exel Logistics, Tibbett and Britten, and Eddie Stobbart have also invested heavily in rail freight facilities for domestic and international traffic. As yet, though, this new type of business is very modest in relation to rail's traditional freight market (see Table A).

Some economists have argued for a long time that road haulage has an unfair advantage over rail freight, making it difficult for rail to compete. They argue that EWS is at a disadvantage because it has to pay the full costs of operating rail freight services. Road freight operators, in contrast, are heavily subsidised, paying considerably less than the social costs of their operations. This particular example of market failure is often referred to as the 'track costs argument'. The basis of this argument is shown in Figure A.

Source: Adapted from the *Mail on Sunday*, 8 March 1998

Figure A How road haulage is effectively subsidised: tax revenue from road users against environmental and public costs in 1994–95

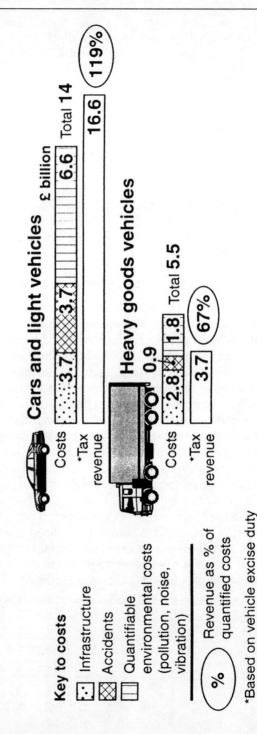

38

Table A Rail freight transport by category of goods (1995–96)

Category of goods	% of total rail freight
Coal	22%
Domestic container goods	19%
Metals	12%
Construction materials	11%
Oil and petroleum	11%
International freight	6%
Other:	
including nuclear waste, chemicals, cars	19%

1. Use Table A to describe the nature of 'rail's traditional freight market'. [2 marks]
2. (a) Explain why major retailers such as Sainsbury's, Safeway and Superdrug have a derived demand for transport. [2 marks]
   (b) State and explain *two* possible reasons why such retailers might switch from road to rail transport. [4 marks]
3. (a) To what extent does the evidence in Figure A support the argument that heavy goods vehicles should be more heavily taxed? [4 marks]
   (b) Why might the information shown in Figure A *not* be particularly accurate? [2 marks]
4. Comment upon the likely effects on transport choice, and on the economy as a whole, of subsidising rail freight. [6 marks]

Chapter Four

Investment in transport

'Spending on motorways and A roads is projected to rise from £1.2 billion this year to £2.9 billion by 2010.' 10-year Transport Plan, July 2000

The nature of transport investment

Investment is the production of goods to be used in the production of other goods and services. In other words, *investment increases the stock of capital in an economy*. In the context of transport, there are two main types of investment decision that have to be taken; these involve the authorization of various types of transport infrastructure and the purchase of vehicles, as implied by the definition of transport in Chapter 1. Economics provides a framework for investment decisions which include:

- Should a new stretch of motorway be built?
- Should a transport business purchase another vehicle or construct a new distribution centre?
- Should a railway station be reopened?
- Should a new rapid transit system go ahead?

An increasing number of decisions in transport are taken by the private sector, using recognized methods of investment appraisal. However, many decisions are still made by the public sector, particularly with respect to transport infrastructure investment, for which private sector methods of appraisal are inappropriate as market prices do not apply. Investment on roads is a rather good example of how the government has had to develop particular procedures in order to allocate resources.

Much transport investment by the public sector is in **public goods**. These are goods which the free market would underproduce or not produce at all. Public goods have two important characteristics:

- **Non-excludability** – the provision of a good or service cannot be made to one person without it being available for others. There is, though, a problem of *free-riders* in so far as it is impossible to prevent external benefits being enjoyed by those who have not paid for the particular good or service.

- **Non-rivalry** – the consumption of a good or service by any one person does not prevent others from enjoying it.

These theoretical characteristics are shown in the box below.

It is interesting to note that the provision of road space is not a pure public good. It is called a **quasi-public good** because there is some element of excludability – only drivers with current licences can legally use roads and people below the age of 17 are excluded along with other non-car-owners from directly using roads. It might also be argued that rivalry occurs through the nature of increased traffic congestion. (See Chapter 6.)

Table 11 shows investment in transport in Great Britain in 1998/99, compared with 1988/89, subdivided between infrastructure and vehicles. The purchase of cars is by far the largest item and – related to this – public sector investment on roads is the greatest infrastructure investment. Private road investment was about 9 per cent of the expenditure made by central and local governments. The resources coming from the private sector will increase in the future, particularly with the construction of the Birmingham Northern Relief Road, the UK's first private motorway, and with new investment in rail vehicles and track.

CLASSIFICATION OF TRANSPORT GOODS

	EXCLUDABLE	NON-EXCLUDABLE
RIVAL	(i) Private goods	(iii) Quasi-private goods
NON-RIVAL	(iv) Quasi-public goods	(ii) Public goods

Examples:
(i)   private cars, airline tickets, airports, Channel Tunnel
(ii)   pavements, lighthouses
(iii)   cheap off-peak travel for pensioners
(iv)   roads

Table 11 Transport investment in 1998/99 (£ million)

	Investment	% change from 1988/89
Road infrastructure		
public	2 847	−7.5
private	267	+323.1
Road vehicles		
cars	34 400	+59.3
other	7 400	+37.0
National rail infrastructure	1 823	+274.3
National rail rolling stock	176	−15.4
Port infrastructure	240	+185.7
Airports infrastructure	680	+133.7

Source: *Transport Statistics,* 2000

Investment in transport infrastructure is:

- long-term in nature, often appraised over a 25–50 year timescale
- expensive, involving vast sums of capital expenditure
- seen as generating various externalities, both positive and negative
- a very important form of capital expenditure by central and local governments.

These characteristics are significant because, for most transport infrastructure expenditure, no direct charge is made to the user. The best example is, of course, the case of roads, where users do not directly pay for the use they make of the network in the UK. Two fundamental questions have to be asked:

- How does the government determine expenditure on roads?
- How does it determine which roads will actually be constructed?

Over the past 30 years or so, economists have used **cost–benefit analysis** (CBA) to provide the answers to questions like these. CBA seeks to establish the overall costs and benefits to society of a particular project such as the construction of a new stretch of motorway. More specifically: *'Cost–benefit analysis is a practical way of assessing the desirability of a project where it is necessary to take a long view and a wide view.'* (Prest and Turvey)

In taking a 'long' view, CBA recognizes the long-term nature of transport infrastructure decisions and seeks to forecast various impor-

---

STEP-BY-STEP PROCEDURES OF COST–BENEFIT ANALYSIS

- Identification of all costs and benefits.
- Enumeration of all costs and benefits; i.e. putting a monetary value on them.
- Assessment of risk and uncertainty in forecasting costs and benefits.
- The effects of time; discounting of costs of benefits to establish net present value.
- Recommendation, based on the calculation of rate of return on capital employed.

---

tant variables over the full length of life of a project, as well as over the very early years. In the case of roads this might be over 25–35 years.

In taking a 'wide' view, CBA seeks to take into account the side-effects of transport infrastructure investment on people, industries, regions and so on.

Some account of externalities, therefore, is built into the CBA objectives and procedures. Whether these externalities can be valued is a rather different matter. The main stages in cost–benefit analysis are shown in the box above.

Since the early 1960s these procedures have been applied to the appraisal of many major transport projects in the UK, and rather more routinely to the construction of motorways and trunk routes. The remainder of this chapter will look at some examples.

The COBA method of appraisal for roads

COBA is the method of appraisal used by the DETR to evaluate new motorway and trunk road schemes. In simple terms it compares the cost of a new road project with the benefits which can be derived by road users. An outline of what is in practice a very complex process is shown in Figure 8.

Why are new roads and motorways built? The simple answer is that they are constructed in order to speed up the flow of traffic and so reduce travel times for car and lorry drivers using them. More specifically, three main types of reduction in user costs are recognized:

- *Journey time savings* – these are normally the most important item in the total benefits from a new road scheme. They are based on the

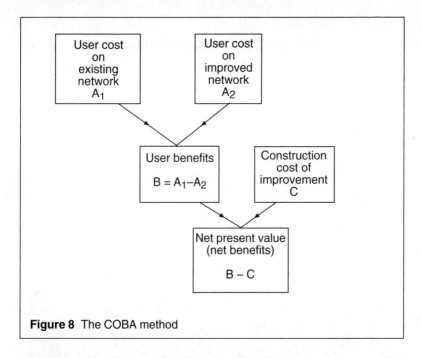

Figure 8 The COBA method

idea that 'time is money'; in other words, the time spent in travelling has a value to the occupants of a vehicle because, if journey times are reduced, the time saved can be used to more meaningful effect. Such time savings are aggregated for all users and a monetary value put on them. This value depends on the purpose of the trip and the mode of transport for work trips – economic activity status is of relevance in determining the value of time for non-work trips.

- *Vehicle operating cost savings* – with the construction of a new stretch of road, vehicles travel not only faster but they can be used in a way which reduces fuel consumption and the wear and tear costs on the brakes, clutch and other parts of the vehicle. These cost savings may be particularly significant for commercial vehicle operators, who require fewer vehicles to do the same amount of work.
- *Accident cost savings* – new motorways and trunk roads are safer to travel on for users, mile for mile, than older roads. Consequently, the probability of experiencing an accident is reduced. The benefits from a reduction in the number and severity of accidents are given a monetary value based on a direct financial cost to individuals, their vehicles and the emergency services, the loss of output of those killed or injured and an allowance for pain, grief and suffering resulting from personal injury or death.

The costs of road accidents

Despite the continued increase in road traffic, it is something of a surprise that the number of road accidents and people killed and seriously injured has actually fallen over the years. Today, the UK has the safest roads in the EU – this is no grounds for complacency, nor is it any consolation for the relatives of the 3,400 road users killed and the 40,000 people seriously injured in road accidents in 1999.

Many types of external costs arise from road accidents. They include

- the human costs of injury or death, including the pain, suffering, grief and value of loss of life in the case of fatal accidents.
- the loss of productive capacity and value of lost working time.
- material damage to vehicles and property
- medical costs
- administrative, police and emergency service costs.

Over the years, economists have sought to put a monetary value onto these costs. This is not easy, although the methodology, which particularly considers the opportunity cost of lost output and the costs to the National Health Service, has become well established. In 1999, the total amount of these external costs was about £3,000m. A substantial proportion (about 40 per cent) consisted of the opportunity cost of lost output. In individual terms, the current cost of someone losing his or her life in a road accident is over £900,000. The cost of someone being seriously injured is about £100,000 per casualty. Both these figures include considerable sums imputed for the 'human costs' of these accidents.

On the expenditure side, COBA takes into account two main costs:

- *Capital costs* – these accrue in the early years of construction of a new road and include the costs of land purchase, road construction, administrative and design costs. With new motorways costing many millions of pounds a mile, this is a major cost item.
- *Maintenance costs* – these are self-explanatory and cover the cost of street lighting, cleaning, maintenance and future resurfacing work.

As shown in Figure 8, the costs and user benefits are then compared to ascertain whether any net value can be gained from the construction of a new road scheme. Where this is so, the **net present value** (NPV) is positive, indicating that there will be some benefit to the community if the road is built. Whether a particular road is constructed, though, will depend on how the NPV in relation to its capital cost compares with other competing schemes. It will also depend on the amount of government expenditure available and the extent to which the road's construction may meet other objectives.

The COBA model has three main practical purposes:

- It establishes whether there is a *need* for a new road scheme.
- It allows *priorities* to be determined. This is normally done on the basis of a rate of return on the capital employed for its construction, also taking into account its length of life.
- It can provide the *basis for a wider discussion* at any public enquiry which may take place.

Criticisms of COBA

Owing to the scale of public expenditure involved and the persistent problem of the demand for new road schemes exceeding the funding that is available, there can be little argument that some method of appraisal is required in order for rational decisions on the construction of new roads to be taken. The cost–benefit approach laid down in COBA can, however, be criticized on various points:

- *It is a user-based method of appraisal* – it looks at whether a new road scheme is needed purely from the perspective of those car users and commercial vehicle operators who will be using it. All new roads, though, have a much wider impact, resulting in various externalities, usually negative, and which are not taken into account in the model. *It is therefore not a fully comprehensive model,* covering all who might be affected by the construction of a new road.
- Over the past 20 years or so, there has been increasing concern over the *environmental effects* of building new roads. As indicated in Table 12, these effects can be substantial and they have provided cause for concern whenever any new road scheme has been proposed. In response to such criticism the Department of Transport now incorporates an assessment of environmental suitability into various stages of the appraisal process, although no monetary value is as yet given to the *negative externalities* involved.
- Certain *value judgements* have to be made. In particular, the valuation of travel time has been the cause of much dispute – a market price is being allocated to something for which no direct charge is made by individuals.

- The **indirect effects** of constructing new roads, particularly in terms of regional development benefits, are not taken into account by the COBA model. There has been a long on-going debate about the extent to which a new road generates a positive economic impact on the area through which it passes. It has also been argued that new roads provide substantial benefits to industrial users that are not included in COBA (see next section for more details).

Government policy for roads in the 1990s

In May 1989, the government published two important Command Papers which had an important bearing on transport policy for roads in the 1990s. These policy statements announced:

- the biggest ever programme of motorway and trunk road construction
- opportunities for the private sector to fund certain new road projects, with clear implications for the way in which users pay for their use of the network.

The main purpose of the *Roads for Prosperity* programme was to reduce inter-urban traffic congestion on the motorway network. In proposing a £12 billion spending package, the government was concerned to give support to industry, while at the same time increasing the opportunities for new development in less favoured regions, particularly those affected by deindustrialization.

The government's plans were undoubtedly prompted by the forecasts of traffic on our roads. The Department of Transport estimated that by the year 2025 road traffic will increase by between 83 and 142 per cent from its 1988 level. It is quite clear that, if this comes about, such an increase in traffic will make congestion on main inter-urban routes significantly worse and unacceptable to users, particularly commercial vehicle and industrial users.

A substantial proportion of the £12 billion expenditure was earmarked for major road-widening schemes on motorways such as the

Table 12 Environmental effects of a new road scheme

Road construction	Loss of valuable land, especially farmland. One mile of motorway needs c. 25 acres of land and 0.25 million tonnes of sand and gravel
Negative externalities	Traffic noise, visual intrusion, loss of amenity once open for use, increased atmospheric pollution. These effects can be particularly severe for those living close to a new road scheme

M1, the M6 and the M25. These motorways and others were expected to be widened to four lanes throughout much of their length. The main stretches of new motorway proposed were between Chelmsford and the M25, relief roads around Manchester and on the approach to the Severn Bridge.

Implementation of this programme was in general confirmed in the White Paper *Policy for Roads for the 1990s*. Reaction to it was predictably mixed. Environmental pressure groups were aghast at the scale of the proposed programme, while the road lobby pressed for even greater expenditure on roads. A very significant government statement in December 1994 was that, once the *Roads for Prosperity* programme had been implemented, there would be no further major new schemes for the foreseeable future.

The *New Roads by New Means* consultation paper attracted considerable attention in the City. This introduced the idea that there could be opportunities for the private sector to invest in roads, a traditional domain for public sector expenditure. Funding of the Channel Tunnel and the Dartford–Thurrock bridge, for example, was in each case from private sources, but this was the first time there had been formal suggestions that users of roads would be required to pay a toll for infrastructure funded by the private sector. Moreover, in October 1989 it was announced that private bidders were being sought to construct a new Birmingham relief road between the M6 and the M54. Two years later, somewhat controversially, the concession to build it was given to an Anglo-Italian joint venture consisting of Trafalgar House and Italstat, the biggest toll road operator in Europe.

A Green Paper, *Paying for Better Motorways,* was published in May 1993. This clearly stated that congestion would continue to worsen unless there was a change in emphasis in the way road users were charged for the use of roads. It stated:

> '... *the introduction of direct charging could be the key to meeting the challenge of congestion ... and would facilitate more private sector involvement in road provision.*'

A charge of around 1½p per mile for cars and 4½p per mile for goods vehicles was suggested as appropriate, although the means by which the toll would be collected was seen as much more of an issue for continuing debate.

Over the last few years, the intentions of the *Roads for Prosperity* programme have been subject to various cutbacks, in part for environmental reasons but more particularly on account of the now widely

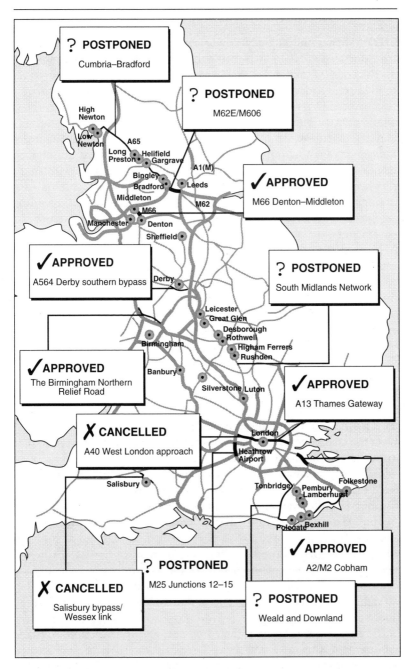

Figure 9 'The road ahead'
Source: *Daily Telegraph*, 29 July 1997

held view that building new roads is not the answer to our deepening transport crisis. One new scheme that has escaped the government's axe is the £300 million Birmingham Northern Relief Road, a privately funded toll road. When constructed, it is expected to relieve congestion on southern sections of the M6, currently a nightmare for those who use it.

After much uncertainty about the place of new road schemes in Labour's transport policy, in July 2000 the government announced its new ten-year transport plan (for details see Chapter 7). Central to this was the announcement of the largest road investment programme since 1989. As the epigraph to this chapter states, spending is expected to increase substantially with the construction of new bypasses and motorway widening schemes (possibly to parts of the M6, M1, M25 and M42). Although the schemes shown in Figure 9 remain 'frozen', there now seems a very good chance that most will proceed, in line with the 'corridors' strategy that is currently being investigated.

By way of perspective, it should be made clear that the plan's emphasis is one of selectivity. There is no suggestion that the major blitz proposed in the 1989 *Roads for Prosperity* programme will be resurrected. It does, however, represent a mini U-turn from a government which at one stage seemed more anti-car and anti-new roads than this ten-year plan might indicate.

The appraisal of motorway projects

Over the last 35 years or so, cost–benefit analysis has been used for the appraisal of many major transport projects in the UK. The most widely applied example is in the appraisal of new motorway and trunk road projects. The methodology used today originated from the case for the M1 motorway.

The M1 motorway study of 1959 was a prototype for the application of CBA to inter-urban road investment. Although not as sophisticated, it has formed the basis for development of the COBA model described above. The main purpose of the M1 study was to justify the decision to construct the London–Birmingham section which had already opened for use by traffic. Table 13 shows a summary of the analysis.

The three cost savings referred to earlier (journey time savings, vehicle operating cost savings and accident cost savings) are shown as benefits. The savings in operating costs were split between two classes of traffic, that diverting to the M1 and that remaining on the

Table 13 Estimated annual costs of, and benefits from, the London–Birmingham motorway (third assignment)

	£000 per annum
Benefits	
To diverted traffic:	
Savings in working time	766
Reduction in vehicle fleets	227
Savings in fuel consumption	18
Savings in other operating costs	200
To traffic remaining on old routes:	
Reduction in vehicle costs	128
Reduction in accident costs:	215
Total	1554
Current costs	
Maintenance of motorway	200
Costs of additional vehicle mileage for traffic diverting to motorway	375
Total	575
Net measured benefits	979

Source: Adapted from Technical Paper 46, Road Research Laboratory, 1960. Crown copyright reproduced with the permission of the Controller of HMSO

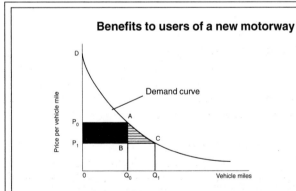

Benefits to users of a new motorway

Assume that DD is the market demand for travel. The effect of opening a new motorway is to reduce travel costs to users from P_0 to P_1 per vehicle mile. As with most demand curves, when the price falls more people will be willing to travel at a reduced price.

At this new reduced price, existing/former travellers will continue to travel. Their aggregate benefit is rectangle P_0ABP_1.

The reduced price also increases the demand for new users wishing to travel. This is known as the *benefit to generated traffic* and is shown by the 'triangle' ABC.

Total traffic benefit = $P_0ABP_1 + ABC$

Consumer surplus increases from DP_0A to DP_1C.

old route, in this case the A45. The M1 study used this classification to show that *consumer surplus* increased when the new motorway was open to traffic. A summary of this important idea is in the boxed item on page 48.

Looking back, it could be argued that investment in *all* forms of transport in the UK has been below what it should have been to ensure a quality transport system to meet the needs of *all* those who want to use it. The new ten-year Transport Plan therefore is seeking to rectify past deficiencies as well as provide new opportunities for transport investment.

KEY WORDS

Investment	Quasi-public good
Public goods	Cost–benefit analysis
Non-excludability	Net present value
Non-rivalry	Indirect effects

Further reading

Bamford, C., (ed.), Chapter 6 in *Economics for AS*, Cambridge University Press, 2000.

Burningham, D., and Davies, J., Chapter 6 in *Green Economics*, 2nd edn, Heinemann, 1999.

Grant, S., and Vidler, C., Unit 16 in *Economics in Context*, Heinemann, 2000.

Munday, S., Chapter 4 in *Markets and Market Failure*, Heinemann, 2000.

Useful websites

DETR – cost benefit analysis approach: www.roads.detr.gov.uk/itwp/appraisal/understanding/index.htm

The European Environment Agency: www.eea.eu.int

Essay topics

1. (a) Explain why it is necessary for the government to apply a cost-benefit approach to the appraisal of new major road schemes in the UK. [10 marks]

(b) Discuss the contribution that the private sector can make to the funding of road investment. [10 marks]
[OCR, November 1998]

2. In Summer 1998, the government announced that the controversial plan to widen part of the M25 motorway was to be fully appraised.

    (a) Explain the basis on which major new road schemes, such as the proposed widening of the M25, are appraised. [10 marks]

    (b) Discuss the likely reasons why the government might *not* implement this particular road widening project. [10 marks]
    [OCR, November 2000]

3. (a) Briefly outline the main *benefits* of constructing new major roads and motorways. [8 marks]

    (b) Comment upon the extent to which *all* of these benefits can be incorporated effectively into a cost-benefit analysis.
    [12 marks]

    [OCR, March 1999]

Data response question

This task is based on a question set by the University of Cambridge Local Examinations Syndicate in 1997. Read the next paragraph and study Tables A and B. Then answer the questions that follow.

The M1–M62 link road

In 1992, the Department of Transport published proposals on two possible options for a new motorway link between the M1 and the M62 in West Yorkshire. These proposals were the outcome of a comprehensive cost–benefit analysis carried out by independent transport consultants. Prior to putting the routes forward for public consultation, an extensive study of the environmental effects was undertaken in which it was stated that 'the preferred route would be the one designed to minimize the adverse environmental effects as far as possible'. Tables A and B summarize a comparison of the two routes, which were named the *purple* and *yellow* routes. The length of the existing route was stated as 23 miles.

Table A Items quantified in the cost–benefit analysis

	Purple route	Yellow route
Length of planned new road	12 miles	10.5 miles
Cost of construction (£ million)	130	135
Forecast percentage changes in traffic on local roads:		
A637	−65 to −55	−55 to −40
A644	−10	−50
A62	+25	+25
A642	−35	−35
Rate of return	'High'	'Very high'

Table B: Items *not* quantified in the cost–benefit analysis

	Purple route	Yellow route
Probable demolition of houses	2	22
No. of houses within 100 metres of new road	65	320
No. of houses fronting main roads which may expect a substantial reduction in traffic	400	600

1. State one strength and one weakness of cost–benefit analysis when used in this context. [2 marks]

2. Use the information provided in Table A to explain why the yellow route gives a higher rate of return than the purple route.
   [4 marks]

3. (a) From Table B, give an example of (i) a negative externality, and (ii) a positive externality. Justify your choices. [4 marks]

(b) Analyse what other negative externalities might have been included in Table B. [4 marks]

4. In 1994, after considerable opposition from local people, the Department of Transport announced that the proposed M1–M62 Link Road would not be constructed. Discuss the likely reasons for this decision. [6 marks]

Chapter Five

Privatization and contestability

'Since the deregulation of public transport, the centre of the city has become a black farce of buses: double deckers, single deckers, even mini-buses, all vying for custom.' Ian Rankin, *Hide and Seek*, No. 2 in The Inspector Rebus series

'While there were many reasons given in the early days about why rail privatization would not work, the critics have been proved wrong.' S. Knight, *Rail Magazine's Guide to Britain's Railways*, 2000

The position before 1979

Prior to the election of Mrs Thatcher's government in 1979, there was very little difference between the two main political parties in their attitude to transport. With the possible exception of road haulage, which had been denationalized in 1953, successive Conservative and Labour administrations had promoted a national transport policy that had sought to obtain 'Co-ordination through Competition'; that is, they had believed the best way to achieve efficiency in transport was through promoting competition, with the private and public sectors competing in certain transport markets.

At the same time, it was also recognized that transport activities should be subject to various forms of regulation and control; particularly for safety reasons, but also to protect the interests of the public sector (often through *quantity licensing*) and to ensure minimum entry control (through *quality licensing*). There was also financial control by government via subsidy provision for bus and rail passenger services and through the control of public expenditure on transport-related projects.

The incoming Thatcher government was faced with emerging transport problems, including:

- increasing levels of subsidy for the railways and local bus services, which was essential in order to retain services
- long-term decline in the bus passenger and rail markets, both of which had almost complete state ownership
- a freight transport market dominated by road, and where rail seemed unable to gain new business
- growing environmental concerns over the impact of increasing transport use

- social concerns over the poor availability of transport services for non-car owners

- a transport network which was experiencing increasing difficulty in coping with the demands placed upon it.

The Thatcher era

By any yardstick, the structural and operational changes in transport since 1979 can only be described as 'radical'. To understand fully their significance, it must be recognized that these changes were carried out by a government which inherited the transport problems listed above and which was also determined to pursue certain economic policies which were based on the following:

- *A deliberate commitment to reduce government involvement in the economy.* A return to market forces was seen as the best way to achieve an efficient allocation of resources.
- *Public sector services providing 'value for money'.* The need for greater accountability was recognized and the government was no longer to be seen as the 'milkcow' which bailed out nationalized industries that persistently lost money.
- *The need to cut back public expenditure.* It was thought necessary to control the growth of aggregate demand so as to limit the deficit on the current account of the balance of payments and to restrict inflationary pressures in the economy.

It was clear that transport, as one of the main areas of the public sector along with the fuel and power industries, would experience the application of new ideas and philosophies. It also became clear that Mrs Thatcher was determined to break down the barriers that protected public sector transport monopolies from competition.

Privatization

In a simple sense, **privatization** refers to a change in ownership of an activity from the public sector to the private sector. Although now a dated term, it is sometimes also referred to as **denationalization**, that is, a return of previously nationalized activities to their former owners. In a modern sense, privatization means rather more than this, as the boxed item on page 58 indicates.

Table 14 lists the main transport privatizations that have taken place and demonstrates how the sale of former public sector assets has been achieved. As it shows, the sale of former public sector transport activities has brought in a substantial amount of money for the Treasury. In the cases of Associated British Ports, British Airways, the

The definition of privatization and its transport application

Denationalization: A change of ownership from public to private sector (e.g. bus services, road freight, airports, ports, air transport, railways)

Deregulation: The removal of barriers to entry, which normally protected the public sector, and the creation of a contestable market (e.g. bus services, air transport)

Franchising: The right to operate a particular service over a stated length of time, with or without public sector subsidy (e.g. some road projects, rail)

Table 14 Transport privatizations in the UK

Date	Company	Nature of sale	£ million
1982	National Freight Company	MBO	52
1983–84	Associated British Ports	Public offering	74
1984	Sealink (from British Rail)	Private sale	66
1986–88	National Bus Company and its subsidiaries	MBO and private sales	325
1987	British Airways	Public offering	900
1987	British Airports Authority	Public offering	1281
1988–	Former PTEs and municipal bus companies	MBO and private sales	n.a.
1994–96	British Rail	Private sales (freight) Franchising (passengers)	n.a.
1996	Railtrack	Public offering	600
1997	London Buses	Route franchising	n.a.
2001 Future?	National Air Traffic System London Underground	Partial sale	

MBO: Management buyout also includes worker management buyouts.
n.a.: not available.
Source: Adapted from H. Hyman, 'Privatization: the facts', Institute of Economic Affairs, 1988

British Airports Authority and Railtrack, it has also provided the public with an opportunity to buy shares. There also has been the selective sale of other British Rail operations, including British Transport Hotels, British Rail Engineering Ltd and the 1983 merger of Seaspeed and HoverLloyd.

There are various benefits of privatization, including:

- a more efficient use of resources
- consumer benefits – wider choice, better quality of service, lower prices
- widening of share ownership
- reduction in the PSBR and benefits for taxpayers.

The arguments for **nationalization** (i.e. state ownership of an activity) are also very pertinent, not least as transport was the first area of the economy to be nationalized in 1947. These arguments include:

- the **natural monopolies** argument – the benefits to consumers of economies of scale and the opportunities presented for product research and development where there is a dominant producer (see Figure 10)
- the externalities argument – where the social benefit exceeds the private benefit of an activity
- distribution/equity arguments – subsidized public sector services can charge below cost and so help those who are less well off
- labour motivation – the idea that labour motivation is higher under state ownership.

The first of these arguments, linked to the case for subsidy, is shown in Figure 10. It has particular relevance for railway operation where capital costs are high and where duplication seemingly serves little purpose. As this figure shows, economies of scale accrue, with the LRAC curve not yet having reached its minimum point. The LRMC is below it, indicating that economies of scale can continue to be gained as output increases.

The dilemma facing natural monopolies is that they cannot survive as profit maximizers (at output Q_m) whilst producing at the social optimum of $P_c Q_2$. Consequently, subsidy is required to support them to operate at this point. Although best applied to rail passenger services, this argument has also been recognized for the provision of both urban and rural bus services, for ferry services and for some unremunerative airline services where there is a **monopoly** operator. Historically, these arguments have been used to justify the protection of such monopolies by means of regulations which prohibit the entry of competitors into the market.

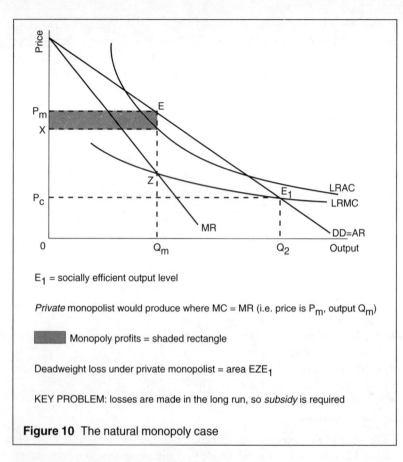

E₁ = socially efficient output level

Private monopolist would produce where MC = MR (i.e. price is P_m, output Q_m)

▓▓▓ Monopoly profits = shaded rectangle

Deadweight loss under private monopolist = area EZE₁

KEY PROBLEM: losses are made in the long run, so *subsidy* is required

Figure 10 The natural monopoly case

Features of a contestable market

The economic rationale underpinning the structural changes to the UK transport industry since 1979 have their origins in the concept of a **contestable market**. This relatively new market structure was promoted by the American economist Baumol in the late 1970s and early 1980s as one which was more flexible than the ones normally found in economics textbooks and one which, where working effectively, required only minimal government regulation and control. First applied to the US domestic airline industry, it has been extensively applied since to many international transport markets, including the UK.

The most important features are as follows:

● Free entry, with no sunk costs for entry into the market. This implies that new and existing market providers will have the same cost structure as in a perfectly competitive market.

- The number and size of firms are irrelevant. If a contestable market contains only a few large firms, any cost differences are a reflection of the quality of their product or a decision by a particular firm to charge a given price.
- Supernormal profits cannot be earned in the long run. Where such profits are being made, then new firms can enter the market and compete them away. This could be on a 'hit and run' basis – in such a case, a firm can see an opportunity, go into the market, collect the gains and then leave at no cost.
- The threat of such competition forces monopolists and oligopolists to offer consumers the benefits that they would receive in a more competitive market structure.
- Firms are productively efficient. Further, the price of the product cannot exceed marginal cost, meeting the condition for Pareto optimality.
- Cross-subsidization is therefore prevented as, since the firm is only earning normal profits, it will go out of business if it sells its products or services at below cost.

The application of contestability to the airline market is particularly interesting as since the 1944 Chicago Convention, and until deregulation, air travel was subject to bi-lateral regulation by governments. In this way, airspace was heavily controlled and market growth restricted. Where deregulation has happened, improved efficiency often occurs and passengers benefit from cheaper fares. A particularly good illustration of this is the way in which low-cost airlines such as easyJet, Ryanair and Go! have entered the market to provide cheaper yet realistic alternatives to established carriers. A further outcome has been the way in which major airlines have formed alliances, once again providing enormous benefits to air travellers (see box).

Deregulation of bus services

The deregulation of bus services started in 1981 with the relatively uncontroversial creation of a contestable market for express bus and coach services (defined as where each passenger travels 30 miles or more). For a time, the state-owned National Travel competed with private bus and coach companies, usually very successfully. The deregulation of local bus services was different in so far as it was accompanied by privatization; the removal of barriers to entry opened up what had traditionally been a protected public sector market but simultaneously, a situation was created whereby all competition was between private sector businesses.

Allies sought in dogfight to rule skies

When the chief executives of British Midland and Singapore Airlines sat huddled next to each other in a Singapore rickshaw earlier this month, it marked a significant development in global aviation. The duo were making a colourful entrance at the Shangri-La Hotel to celebrate their membership of the world's largest and ever-growing airline grouping, Star Alliance (see below). Together with the bosses of Star's other member carriers, it was easy to see why such images would send the jitters through rival alliances, including One World, led by British Airways.

British Midland is the second biggest airline at Heathrow, while Singapore Airlines is the world's most profitable carrier and a key strategic player in South East Asia. Fellow Star members American Airlines and Lufthansa operate Trans-Atlantic and German flights from Heathrow. As a consequence, the alliance has an increasingly tight grip on the world's busiest international airport. Overall it controls 24 per cent of all available slots at Heathrow, British Airways' hub. British Midland controls two thirds of these slots.

Heathrow has always been a battleground for airlines desperate to hold on to their precious slots. The airport though is itself becoming an even more valuable asset in the alliance scenario as it competes more vigorously with the likes of Frankfurt (Lufthansa), Schipol (KLM) Charles de Gaulle (Air France) and Vienna (Austrian Airlines). Because of slot constraints, alliances help airlines to operate services through their partners without committing their own aircraft, thus reducing costs.

British Airways (BA) has proved unable to use its dominant position at Heathrow, where it holds 38 per cent of all slots, to its full potential. It has tried to merge with American Airlines and more recently with KLM but on both occasions, the marriage has had to be aborted. BA's new chief executive Rod Eddington, named only yesterday, will be keenly aware of the lack of progress as he steps into his new job. Rival alliance Star is becoming a very competitive force on his home patch.

Star Alliance

Air Canada	Air New Zealand
All Nippon Airways	Ansett Australia
Austrian Airlines	British Midland
Lauda Air	Lufthansa
Mexicana Air	SAS – Scandinavian Airlines
Singapore Airlines	Thai Airways
Tyrolean Airways	Varig
United Airlines	

Adaptation: *The Times*, 26 April 2000

The economic logic underpinning deregulation was that, despite this protection and ever-increasing subsidies, the industry and its market continued to decline (see box below). The removal of **cross-subsidization** was a particularly important consideration.

Cross-subsidization is *internal* to the business and has been practised widely in transport. It involves a situation whereby profits earned in one part of an operation (e.g. urban bus services) are used to support loss-making services (e.g. semi-urban or rural services). This practice results in companies providing a network of services, rather than just those services that pay their way.

It is argued that cross-subsidization is inefficient. The basis for this claim is that it leads to higher costs and fares in some areas, yet lower costs in other areas are not passed on to passengers through lower fares. It is therefore an example of *implicit taxation*. Cross-subsidization can also be wasteful – marginal services may be supported too heavily, generating dubious benefits in relation to their costs.

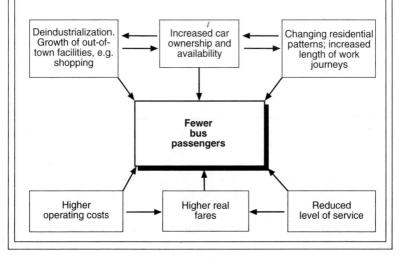

The decline of bus passenger transport

The bus passenger market has been in long-term decline over the last 30–40 years. The main cause of this decline has been the growth in car ownership levels, but, as the diagram below indicates, there are other reasons related to developments in the UK economy and operational causes which are much more specific to the bus industry. The outcome is quite clearly one of fewer bus passengers.

Transport Act 1985 – the deregulation and privatization of local bus services

Scope	All local bus services in Great Britain, excluding London; vast majority of these services operated by the public sector
Main provisions:	
Deregulation	Abolition of the road service licence requirement which restricted who could operate local bus services and what services could be provided
Privatization	Reorganization and sale of public sector bus operators. National Bus Company subsidiaries to be sold to management teams and others. PTEs and municipal operators to be set 'at arms length' from their local authorities with provision for their future sale
Operator's licence	To become the only legal requirement for entry into this market; consistent with the principle of a contestable market
Competitive tendering	Introduced for routes which were to be subsidized by newly constituted PTEs; all other routes to become 'commercial'
Other	Concessionairy fare schemes to remain available, with safeguards to protect rural services; trial corridors with competitive tendering to be set up in London, otherwise no change in the capital for the time being

Subsidy, on the other hand, is *external* to the business; it is paid by central and local governments to protect loss-making services. National transport policy has sought to get 'value for money' where subsidy is paid and has increasingly questioned its need. The days are gone when local government was prepared to write blank cheques to keep bus services on the road and to support services which nobody wanted or used.

Table 15 summarizes the general impact of bus deregulation. It presents a mixed picture. The deregulation of express coach services has been relatively successful and its impact was used to justify the similar deregulation of local bus services outside London. The reality of this second deregulation has been somewhat different from what had been

Table 15 The impact of deregulation

Express coach services (1980 Transport Act)	Significant early market entry, product innovation, fare reductions, improved service levels
	then
	Sequence of market exits, service consolidation, higher frequencies and more competitive fares on main routes
Local bus services (1985 Transport Act)	Increased number of operators, extensive competition in some areas, reduced subsidy, continued fall in number of passengers, mergers/takeovers and market exits
	then
	Increasing real fare levels, continued drop in number of passengers, fewer new vehicles, deteriorating employment conditions, reduced subsidy and increasing concentration of ownership

expected. *In particular, there has been concern as to whether the market really is contestable – in other words, how well does the theory of contestable markets hold up in local bus transport?*

This question is answered to some extent in Table 16. Following privatization in 1986, many local authority, PTE-owned and National Bus Company-owned companies were sold to management/employee teams through management buyouts (MBOs). Few now remain, largely as a result of them having been sold on to one or other of the so-called 'major groups'. For example, Stagecoach now owns GM South and Busways in Manchester and Newcastle-upon-Tyne respectively. First Bus, created in 1996 through the merger of Badgerline and Grampian Regional Transport, has now overtaken Stagecoach with a series of further acquisitions (see Table 17). West Midlands Travel and National Express have also amalgamated. The outcome is that many companies who entered the local bus market in 1986 have now left it, in many cases selling out for a good profit to one of the major groups.

These large companies have shown little inclination to compete directly with each other. Geographically, they are each strong in particular parts of the country. Stagecoach, for instance, has substantial control of the market in South Wales and Scotland. First Bus, its largest rival, has its main operations in East Anglia, West Yorkshire and other parts of South Wales and Scotland. Where their operations

Table 16   Market share of bus operators, 1999

	(by turnover)
First Group	23.0%
Stagecoach	16.4%
Arriva	13.6%
Go-Ahead	6.5%
National Express Group	6.2%
MTL	2.1%
Smaller groups	3.1%
Management-owned	7.3%
Municipals	6.7%
Independents	14.8%
Employee-owned	0.3%

It is difficult to make comparisons with earlier years due to the many ownership changes, take-overs and mergers. First Group especially has emerged very clearly as market leader since 1995 when Stagecoach had the largest market share. The three- and five-firm concentration ratios have both increased as well since 1995.

Source: *Bus Industry Monitor*, September 1999

Table 17   First Group companies

Bus companies

First Aberdeen	First Leicester
First Beeline	First Lowland
First Bradford	First Mainline
First Bristol	First Manchester
First Calderdale	First Midland Bluebird
First Capital	First Midland Red
First CentreWest	First Provincial
First Cymru	First PMT
First Eastern Counties	First Southampton
First Essex	First Wessex
First Glasgow	First Western National
First Huddersfield	First York
First Leeds	

Train companies

First Great Eastern	First North Western
First Great Western	

Airport
Bristol International Airport plc (sold in December 2000)

do encroach upon each other, then in general the competition is really limited; in contrast all major groups normally take a predatory attitude to smaller companies which try to steal market share.

The trend towards increased concentration of ownership shown in Table 16 has not gone unnoticed by the Office of Fair Trading (OFT), which has been asked to investigate claims of unfair practices in Oxford, Darlington and Chesterfield, amongst others. The OFT is seeking to protect the interests of passengers, whilst at the same time ensuring that all firms in the market do not go beyond the accepted basis for competition.

Structurally, the market is somewhat enigmatic in so far as the following:

- At a local level, it is still in theory *contestable*. New firms should be able to enter the market and remain there if incumbent operators are making above normal profits. In practice, the tactics of established companies, both fair and unfair, make such entry problematic with few new entrants now surviving in a harsh competitive business. At best, these new entrants might hope to pick up subsidized routes to help them remain in this business.
- As a consequence, in many towns and cities, established operators have a **local monopoly** whereby they are responsible for a high percentage share of their local market. In such cases their only competitors will be very small and providing a narrow range of services. In other places, the market takes the form of a **duopoly**, with two large companies battling to retain or gain market share.
- At a national level, the industry is developing clear signs of being an **oligopoly** as evidenced by increasing concentration ratios. For example, Table 16 indicates three- and five-firm concentration ratios of 53 per cent and 66 per cent respectively in 1999; by way of comparison, these were 31 per cent and 43 per cent in 1995. First Group has now clearly established its place as market leader. The major players in the bus market have also emerged as powerful forces in the more recently privatized rail passenger market (see below).

The following conclusions can be made about the outcome of local bus service deregulation:

- The market for local bus services has continued to decline, with the greater losses of patronage being in the metropolitan counties.
- The market in London is up slightly, arguably for non-transport reasons.
- The degree of competition for routes has been variable – intense pressure on some routes, no competition on others.
- Many off-peak services have been withdrawn.

Logistics – an emerging oligopoly

An interesting, and in some respects not well-known, example of an oligopolistic transport market is that of firms providing what is known as 'third party logistics services.' These services involve managing the supply chains of clients, including retailers, manufacturers and almost any other type of business which has a regular distribution need. In particular, this involves the provision of freight transport and warehousing services; it can also include the assembly of raw materials and parts (say for a vehicle assembly plant) and the collection of goods from a range of suppliers (say for a grocery retailer).

The growth in demand for logistics services has been consistently strong over the last 15 years or so and as a consequence, there has been the spectacular growth of firms such as the ones shown below.

	Turnover (1999) (£m)
Exel Logistics	1801
Ocean Group	1770
Tibbett and Britten Group	1312
Hays Logistics	895
Securicor Omega Logistics	640
Wincanton Logistics	603
TNT (UK) Ltd	600
Christian Salvesen plc	591

The industry now displays all the signs of an oligopoly. For example,

– customer service, rather than price, is an important reason why some firms continue to pick up new contracts.
– increasingly, there are high set-up costs which act as a barrier to the entry of new firms.
– there is increasing evidence of collusion between some of the largest firms when new contracts are offered (for example, Exel Logistics and Tibbett and Britten securing a lucrative contract with Marks and Spencer in May 2000).
– companies are seeking to increase market share through establishing a brand image, which is a form of non-price competition.

All of the firms listed above have experienced considerable growth since the mid-1980s. Exel (following the merger of Exel Logistics and the Ocean Group) is the market leader and a very important business in global markets. Others below them in this table have experienced substantial growth, either from within or through acquisition. The four and six firm concentration ratios have increased consistently over the years and can be expected to do so over the next few years.

- The annual subsidy paid to operators by local authorities has been falling in recent years. In 1998/99, it was £222 million, less than half of its 1986 level.
- Fare levels are higher in real terms and rising at a faster rate than the cost for using a car.

Whether or not deregulation has resulted in a better allocation of resources is difficult to assess. Most of the evidence points to this *not* being the case. Typical of the general perception is Ian Rankin's view at the beginning of this chapter. It was of particular significance for London in late 1993 when surprisingly, the proposed deregulation of services was scrapped. In time, it has been replaced by a system of tendering for route franchises, with private companies competing for them as they have become available. As expected, the large operators have been particularly successful in securing these, whilst London Transport Buses has determined supply side competition and network planning. Arguably, it has enabled London to get the best of both worlds. Many would argue that this approach would have been better than deregulation for our major conurbations and cities.

Rail privatization in Great Britain

As Chapter 7 will show, rail has a very important part to play in the future transport network of the country. This is now clearly recognized in national transport policy, incorporating both passenger and freight traffic. It has not always been the case; indeed, the main problem which politicians and railway managers have had to address over the last 40 years is that of the role and place of railways in the domestic transport system.

In the early 1960s, the now infamous Dr Beeching tried to put railways on a commercial footing and was given a mandate 'to make them pay'. After a tremendous spate of closures, the principle of providing subsidies for passenger services was introduced in the 1968 Transport Act. The escalating burden of this subsidy resulted in the Serpell Inquiry of 1983. Its purpose was to investigate the services that could be provided for various levels of subsidy and once more its finding raised serious doubts over rail's future in a road-dominated transport network.

Eventually in the early 1990s, the Conservative government saw privatization as the answer to rail's problem, whilst recognizing that some subsidy would have to be paid for most passenger services, albeit on a declining basis. This controversial privatization turned out to be a complex issue and was different from other transport privatizations due to the following:

- The nature of railway operations, whereby there was dedicated track and infrastructure on which passenger and freight trains operated.
- British Rail at the time of privatization was a loss-making business. Although freight just about covered its costs, many essential passenger services did not and required substantial subsidies from central and local government for their continuation.
- Safety was an overriding consideration – it was inconceivable that commercial pressures could compromise the safety of rail users.
- There was no precedent in so far as the UK was the first major country to privatize its rail network.

After much deliberation and debate, privatization proceeded on the basis of the virtual separation of infrastructure from train operations, an approach strongly promoted by the Adam Smith Institute. The 1993 Railways Act, which had a difficult passage through Parliament, was a complex piece of legislation. Controversial clauses to introduce 'open access' competition against passenger franchise holders were modified so leaving train operating companies with an opportunity to establish a monopoly to run services on their particular routes. Also significant was the parliamentary decision to retain through ticketing and the national sale of tickets, so avoiding the much feared airline style of ticketing practices. Largely based on this Act, the structure of UK's rail system is shown in the box on page 66.

Market structures

The transport market provides some interesting applications of the theoretical models which have been developed in economics. For example:

- Railtrack is a *monopoly* supplier of network services to the passenger and freight train operators. They have no choice and, in certain respects, have to accept the track charges made by Railtrack. The Rail Regulator can step in to intervene if these charges are regarded as excessive. More correctly, Railtrack has a natural monopoly – it is a single supplier by law. Figure 10 showed how in this case, the LRAC has not reached its minimum point. As the LRMC curve is below it, economies of scale continue to be gained. Supernormal or monopoly profits can also be earned in the long run as the shaded box indicates. Profits have been a particularly controversial issue (in 1999, for example, pre-tax profits of £428 million were made on a turnover of £2573 million). Critics have argued that these profits should be fully re-invested in new projects and not returned by

THE PRIVATIZED RAIL STRUCTURE

Railtrack
The monopoly owner of railway infrastructure (i.e. the track, signalling, stations, depots, bridges and tunnels). Initially in public ownership but successfully privatized in May 1996. Derives its income from train operating companies (TOCs) and freight users of the network. Retains ownership of 14 major stations whilst leasing out others to TOCs. Funding major new investment projects and upgrades.

Train operating companies (TOCs)
The companies operating the 25 passenger franchises, most of which receive some form of subsidy. Recent ownership changes have seen major bus operators increasing their hold in the market. Further increase in concentration of ownership seems likely.

Freight operators
English, Welsh and Scottish Railway (EWS) has over 80 per cent of the market. Freightliner and a small number of other private operators have the rest.

Rolling stock companies (ROSCOs)
Lease passenger locomotives and rolling stock to the TOCs. Controversial sale of original companies to Stagecoach Holdings (Porterbrook) and HSBC (Eversholt). Angel is the other main one. New entrants likely as TOCs become more prepared to invest.

Office of the Rail Regulator (ORR)
Ensures competition is fair and protects interests of passengers. Has important role in regulating how Railtrack acts, particularly with respect to charges.

Strategic Rail Authority (SRA)
Set up in 2000, this important new body has a wide-ranging mandate to promote the better use of the railways within an integrated transport policy (see Chapter 7). Has other functions including the assessment of future investment and drawing up policies for competition between TOCs. Also taken over the franchising work of OPRAF.

Railtrack to its shareholders. A further theoretical consideration is that Railtrack is not producing at the social optimum ($P_c Q_2$) as its profits would not be maximized at this point.

- The TOCs and EWS are to some extent monopolies. On the passenger side, many TOCs face no competition from 'open access' operators, which in theory can enter the market a few years after the franchise has been awarded. The high sunk costs of entry and the limited revenue prospects clearly serve as relevant barriers to entry, protecting the interest of the franchisee. In a very small number of cases (for example Hull Trains v GNER and Northern Spirit v Virgin West Coast) there is competition, but this invariably results in the franchisee having a very substantial share of the market. What is more common is for franchised TOCs to compete where there is geographical overlap in their routes (for example WAGN v GNER between Peterborough and London, and Silverlink Trains v Virgin West Coast between Birmingham and London). For freight, market entry may appear easier, although again the high costs of entry serve to deter would-be competitors to EWS.

Most TOCs operating on main-line routes are able to exploit their monopoly power through **price discrimination**. In particular, they seek to increase revenue where their market can be segmented into sectors with different price elasticities of demand. The best example of this is between the peak and the off-peak market, which tend to be price inelastic and price elastic respectively. A standard open return between Leeds and London Kings Cross cost £114 in November 2000; the most expensive off-peak fare, a saver ticket, was £64, but holders of this ticket could only travel on weekdays after 9.00 a.m. and at weekends. Even cheaper fares, as little as £13.50, were available for travellers able to pre-book travel together and who were prepared to restrict when they travelled. In this way, the market is separated, providing the operator with the opportunity to increase revenue. Increasingly, the market for rail travel is exhibiting the same tendencies as in airline operations.

Figure 11 shows the equilibrium price and output of a price discriminating monopolist. If the monopolist were to charge a single price P_1 where MC = MR, then a loss would be made. This is indicated in the shaded area. By price discriminating, the monopolist is making use of the fact that some consumers are prepared to pay above this price, for example business travellers living in Leeds who have early morning appointments in London. At prices above P_1, the monopolist is seeking to erode its consumer surplus if consumers were only paying this price. By converting this into producer surplus, the monopolist can increase

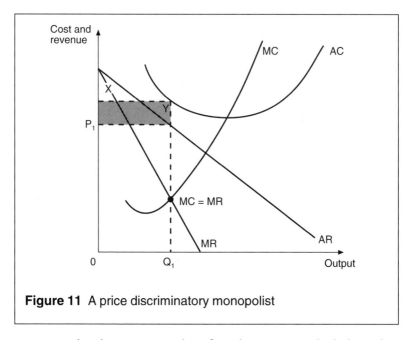

Figure 11 A price discriminatory monopolist

revenue and make supernormal profits. The extent to which this policy is successful depends upon the respective sizes of the two triangles X and Y in Figure 11. If X is larger in area than Y (as shown), then the monopolist will make some supernormal profits. In rail travel the analysis is complicated by the loss-making nature of most of the franchises (see Figure 12). Even so, the Rail Regulator has to keep an eye on the pricing policies of the TOCs to ensure that customers as a whole are not being exploited.

The major passenger train operators are shown in the box on page 70. As this indicates, many of the franchises are due for renewal in the near future. Competition for some such as GNER's East Coast Main Line and Northern Spirit's Trans-Pennine routes is expected to be such that the existing holders may be forced out. In most cases though, as the case of Chiltern Railways indicates, the franchise holder is in a strong position to keep its operation for an extended period.

In the time that franchises have been let, there have been important ownership changes. Major bus operators now have a strong control in the rail passenger business. First Group especially has a substantial interest, as does the National Express Group. Arriva has recently taken over two struggling franchises and Stagecoach seems determined to increase its presence in this market. As in local bus service operations, the strength of these companies is likely to be a formidable

Northern Spirit, part of the Arriva Group, operates trains over a wide area in West and North Yorkshire, Humberside, Lancashire and Cumbria. It receives extensive subsidy for all services, especially those serving rural areas and for socially necessary routes.

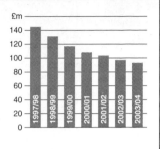

GNER, part of Sea Containers, operates flagship services from Scotland, the North East and West Yorkshire to Kings Cross on the East Coast Main Line. When its franchise comes up for renewal, the level of subsidy provided will be minimal.

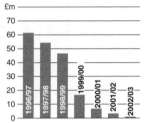

Virgin West Coast operates trains between Glasgow, the North West, the West Midlands and London Euston. From 2002/03, it will have to pay an increasing premium to operate these services. The company is investing heavily in new trains.

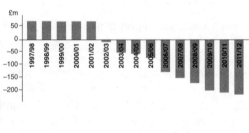

Gatwick Express, part of the National Express Group, was the first franchise to be awarded on the basis of premium payments for the full duration of the contract. A highly successful operation.

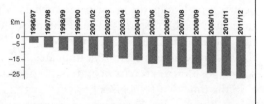

Figure 12 Subsidy and premium: payments profile of four TOCs

Source: *Britain's Railways*, EMAP, 2000

barrier to the entry of new companies as well as a deterrent to would-be open access competitors.

The major rail passenger groups in 2000

Major group	Franchises held	Expiry date
Arriva plc	Merseyrail Electrics	April 2004
	Northern Spirit	April 2004
Connex Rail	Connex South Central*	May 2003
	Connex South East	October 2011
First Group plc	First Great Eastern	April 2004
	First Great Western	February 2006
	First North Western	April 2004
GB Railways Ltd	Anglia Railways	April 2004
GNER Holdings	Great North Eastern Railway†	April 2003
Go-Ahead Group plc	Thameslink Rail	April 2004
	Thames Trains	April 2004
M40 Trains Ltd	Chiltern Railways	August 2020
National Express Group	Central Trains	April 2004
	Gatwick Express	April 2011
	Midland Main Line	April 2006
	ScotRail Railways	April 2004
	Silverlink Train Services	September 2004
Prism Rail plc	Cardiff Railway Company	April 2004
	LTS Rail Ltd	May 2011
	Wales and West Passenger Trains Ltd	April 2004
	West Anglia GNR Ltd	April 2004
Stagecoach Holdings plc	Island Line Ltd	October 2001
	South West Trains	February 2003
	(49% shareholding in Cross Country Trains Ltd West Coast Trains Ltd)	
Virgin Trains Ltd	Cross Country Trains Ltd	March 2012
	West Coast Trains Ltd	March 2012

* Future franchise awarded, in November 2000, to VEO Rail
† Franchise currently being renegotiated

Source: Adapted from *The Comprehensive Guide to Britain's Railways*, EMAP Active,

Rail freight

On the freight side, British Rail's three freight companies were eventually sold to the English, Welsh and Scottish Railway (EWS) for £225 million in 1996. Controversially at the time, this international consortium's principal partner is the US-owned Wisconsin Central International. Its pledge at the time of the sale was to treble its business by 2005 by breaking down the traditional market barriers which had tended to favour road haulage and distribution. EWS later acquired Rail Express Systems, whose main customer was the Post Office, and Railfreight Distribution, which was responsible for intermodal rail freight services through the Channel Tunnel.

EWS is now responsible for over 80 per cent of the UK's rail freight business. The other main operator is Freightliner, which is responsible for the rail-borne transport of containers between deep sea ports and a network of inland terminals and for their internal distribution between terminals in the UK. After substantial subsidy from the government, Freightliner was privatized through a management buy-out. The remaining operators are very small: they are Direct Rail Services, a subsidiary of British Nuclear Fuels, Mendip Rail and GB Freight, a subsidiary of Anglia Railways.

The principle of contestability embedded in the 1993 Railways Act makes provision for 'open access rights', whereby independent rail freight companies can operate freight trains on the Railtrack network. Entry into this market though requires substantial sunk costs to be available and for would-be entrants to agree appropriate track-cost charges with Railtrack. To date these have constituted formidable barriers to entry.

As Chapter 1 indicated, rail freight's share of the domestic freight market had fallen to less than 6 per cent of freight moved (7 per cent in terms of tonne-kilometres) at the time of privatization. Moreover, the prospects for EWS especially seemed pessimistic, with a steady 2–3 per cent fall per annum being predicted. It is therefore quite remarkable to record that under private ownership, rail freight has enjoyed a revival in its fortunes. By 1999, the tonne-kilometres carried had increased by 30 per cent to 18.4 billion, with further increases expected in line with EWS's targets.

The main sources of growth have been twofold, both closely linked to the general growth in the UK economy. These are:

- a growth in international traffic via the Channel Tunnel, in particular taking advantage of the EU-promoted Trans European Rail Freight Freeways (TERFFs) to Italy, Spain and central Europe

- a growth in domestic intermodal traffic moved by Freightliner, up 20 per cent since privatization.

In contrast, the traditional movement of bulk materials, particularly coal, has continued to decline although there has been some modest growth in iron and steel traffic.

The key to rail's recent success has been the substantial investment in rail vehicles and rolling stock by both EWS and Freightliner. For EWS, the most noticeable feature has been the arrival in the UK of over 200 Canadian-built freight locomotives and a massive programme of investment in 2500 UK-produced wagons. Freightliner has also invested heavily in new container-carrying wagons and in upgrading its rail vehicles, road vehicles and handling equipment. In addition, new tracks are being laid to provide freight services to new customers close to the rail network and upgrades are taking place of tracks to the main east coast container ports.

The response of major logistics companies and their customers has also been positive, consistent with the government's promotion of a more sustainable national transport policy (see Chapter 7). The dynamic Tibbett & Britten Group has emerged as a new powerful force, along with Exel, which in 2000 merged with MSAS Logistics to form a global logistics operation. 'Steady Eddie' (Eddie Stobart) has also moved into rail freight, building a relationship with Direct Rail Services. In addition, high profile retailers such as Argos, Safeway, Sainsbury's, Superdrug and Tesco have switched small volumes of primary distribution traffic, particularly from outside the UK, to rail freight from road. Overall this is a very positive outcome entirely consistent with the government's objective of making a more effective use of the rail freight network.

Has privatization succeeded?

At the time of privatization it was believed that the following benefits would accrue:

- Increased efficiency through reducing costs and cutting out waste.
- There would be more concern for customer needs.
- Management freedom would produce a market-led service.
- Subsidy from central and local government would be reduced.
- New investment would be provided from both Railtrack and the TOCs.

The last two benefits have particular interest to economists and can be applied to determine whether privatization has been successful.

When taking up the franchises, the TOCs were left in no doubt that subsidy payments would fall over time and in a few cases, a premium would have to be paid to the government (see Figure 12). In 1998/99, the total subsidy paid was £1544 million, almost 30 per cent below the pre-privatization level. The economics of running passenger trains on the current network is such that subsidy is absolutely essential to retain existing services and frequencies with few exceptions, although a modest decrease is likely to continue in the future.

Under state ownership the railways suffered from many years of under-investment. Under private ownership, Railtrack has committed substantial resources to major development projects such as reconstructing the West Coast Main Line, a long-awaited and essential Channel Tunnel rail link and improvements to certain parts of the East Coast Main Line. Smaller projects have been to increase capacity on other routes and, in time, even construct lines on sections of track closed by Dr Beeching in the mid-1960s. Rail passengers have also benefited from station improvements across the entire network.

Less satisfactory for passengers has been the disappointing performance in terms of punctuality, which is defined as whether a train arrives within ten minutes of the published time at its end destination. The TOCs are given monthly performance targets which are monitored on an annual basis by the Strategic Rail Authority. Most are currently performing below this target and in the vast majority of cases, performed less well in 1999/2000 than in the previous year. Some TOCs like Chiltern Railways, First Great Eastern and ScotRail have consistently recorded high levels of punctuality – this is not the case with Virgin Cross Country where punctuality is the lowest of all, typically 75 per cent against a target of 90 per cent.

Whether privatization has succeeded is a difficult question to answer. In market terms, in contrast to local bus services, there has been a 25 per cent increase in passenger business and a 30 per cent increase in freight business since privatization. There has also been a fall in subsidy for passenger services and substantial new and planned investment in infrastructure way beyond the scope of the public sector. In these terms, it has surely been successful. In other respects, largely from a customer standpoint, privatization has not solved the daily problem of getting to work on time and at a price that most workers can afford.

In autumn 2000, the rail network experienced unprecedented problems as a consequence of the Hatfield rail crash on the GNER-operated East Coast Main Line, and extensive flooding, both of which contributed to tremendous chaos for passengers and freight. Of most concern to passengers was the issue of rail safety, amidst revelations that large parts of the network were deficient from this standpoint. Railtrack came in for heavy criticism and new doubts were being expressed over the structure explained earlier in this chapter. What has been particularly alarming has been the loss of passenger aand freight traffic to road as a consequence of the severe disruption to the network following the Hatfield crash. Although in some respects 'the critics have been proved wrong', in other respects it is very clear that there are severe weaknesses in this most controversial of all transport privatizations.

The rail safety crisis

As previously stated, at the time of privatization there was considerable concern over the issue of safety by those objecting to the sell off. The fear was that there was a conflict between achieving punctuality (and so avoiding fines) and operating safely. These fears intensified with fatal accidents at Clapham and Hatfield, both of which involved fast-moving passenger trains. What emerged from the Hatfield crash of October 2000 was that the cause was a cracked rail – the aftermath was an even more worrying revelation that large parts of the network were in urgent need of repair by Railtrack. Many speed restrictions were then imposed by Railtrack, throwing the whole network into a state of chaos.

From a wider perspective, there have been two important consequences.

- Public confidence in the rail network has been badly shaken. So much so that on some services passenger loadings were down by up to 50 per cent; thousands of freight trains were cancelled and EWS was very concerned that hard-won business was now being lost to road transport. Both, if they persist, are bad news for the Government's pursuit of a sustainable transport policy. (See chapter 7 for details.)
- Considerable concern that no single body in the privatized rail structure has overall responsibility for rail safety. The issue is further complicated by Railtrack's use of many different contractors to carry out safety work on the track.

The scale of the problem is that it has cast a shadow over the emerging success of rail privatization. It has also cast grave doubts over the complicated structure that currently provides rail services in the UK. Increased Government regulation, affecting Railtrack especially, seems inevitable. Arguably, deregulation in this case has not been appropriate.

KEY WORDS

Privatization	Cross-subsidization
Denationalization	Local monopoly
Nationalization	Duopoly
Natural monopolies	Oligopoly
Monopoly	Price discrimination
Contestable market	

Further reading

Bamford, C., (ed.), Chapter 3 in *Economics for AS*, Cambridge University Press, 2000.

Grant, S., Chapter 4 in Stanlake's *Introductory Economics*, 7th edn, Longman, 2000.

Griffiths, A., and Ison, S., Chapters 1–4 in *Business Economics*, Heinemann, 2001.

Griffiths, A., and Wall, S., Chapter 12 in *Applied Economics*, 8th edn, Longman, 2000.

Useful website

Office of the Rail Regulator (ORR): www.rail-reg.gov.uk

Essay topics

1. (a) With specific reference to a transport mode of your choice, explain the advantages of privatization. [8 marks]
   (b) 'Many MPs saw rail privatization as an increasing drain on tax revenue ... but these warnings have turned out to be wide of the mark.' (The Economist Election Briefing, 1996) Comment on this view of the early effects of the privatization of Britain's railways. [12 marks]

   [OCR, March 1999]

2. (a) Explain the economic reasons for the deregulation of local bus services in the UK. [8 marks]
   (b) 'The Government believes that regulatory changes to bus services are needed in the future to achieve a better allocation of resources in urban transport.' (G. Strang, Transport Secretary, 1997) Discuss this view that greater regulation is now needed. [12 marks]

   [OCR, March 2000]

3. In Summer 1998, the annual report of the Rail Franchise Director stated that the operating performance of the 25 passenger train companies was very unsatisfactory and in many respects unacceptable.
   (a) Explain why rail passenger services in Great Britain were privatized in the early 1990s. [10 marks]
   (b) Discuss the extent to which the above view of the Rail Franchise Director is a fair assessment of the impact of rail privatization. [10 marks]
   [OCR, November 2000]
4. Explain how each of the following market structures are of relevance in the transport sector in the UK:
   (a) natural monopoly [5 marks]
   (b) monopoly [5 marks]
   (c) oligopoly [5 marks]
   (d) a contestable market. [5 marks]

Data response question

The following task was set by OCR in November 1998. Read the data and then answer the questions that follow.

Bus deregulation – a contestable market?

The main economic principle which has underpinned the deregulation of local bus services has been to create a contestable market. Following deregulation in 1986, many small bus operators were formed. Some of these were from management or employee buyouts of the former publicly-owned National Bus Company subsidiaries and municipal transport operators. Other new companies which entered the market were small private operators of other types of bus and coach services.

The structure of the bus industry has changed since the early days of deregulation, as Table A below indicates. Whether or not the market is now contestable is a matter of debate amongst economists, who fear that the changes in structure shown in Table A provide potential for anti-competitive behaviour. The Monopolies and Mergers Commission (MMC) and the Office of Fair Trading (OFT) have also expressed concern at these trends and at the business practices and behaviour of some of the large bus operators.

Table A Market shares[1] of bus companies, 1989–95[1]

Company	1989	1992	1995
Major groups			
Stagecoach	3.9	4.9	13.4
First Bus[2]	3.7	6.2	12.6
British Bus	2.8	3.4	8.8
Total major groups	**10.4**	**14.5**	**34.8**
Emerging groups			
National Express/West Midlands Travel	0	5.9	7.7
Go-Ahead Group	1.7	1.7	4.3
Cowie Group	0.6	0.6	3.5
MLT	0	0	3.2
SB Holdings	0	0	3.3
Others[3]			
Publicly-owned	30.4	18.1	7.5
Other privately owned companies	56.9	59.2	35.7
	100	100	100

[1] Percentage share of the market based on income from fares

[2] Badgerline and Grampian Regional Transport before 1995

[3] Includes employee-owned, management-owned, independent bus companies and London Buses

1. (a) Using Table A, state which of the *major groups* has experienced the fastest rate of growth in market share
    (i) between 1989 and 1992 [1 mark]
    and
    (ii) between 1992 and 1995. [1 mark]
   (b) The data shown in Table A is based on income from fares (Note [1]). Give *two* other measures of market growth which could be used to show the changes in market share from 1989 to 1995. [2 marks]
2. (a) Use the information in Table A to describe *two* ways in which 'the structure of the bus industry has changed since the early days of deregulation'. [2 marks]

   (b) Briefly explain *one* likely economic reason for each of these changes in structure. [4 marks]

3. (a) Explain the characteristics of a contestable market. [4 marks]

   (b) Discuss why economists, the MMC and OFT are concerned about 'the business practices and behaviour of some of the large bus operators'. [6 marks]

Chapter Six

The economics of traffic congestion

'Jam today, road pricing tomorrow.' The Economist, 1997

The problem of congestion

Congestion is an all too familiar feature of most transport networks. It occurs when there is too much traffic for existing capacity so that the *actual journey times taken by transport users are in excess of their normal expectations*. Consequently it is inefficient and costly to transport users. In 1989, the CBI Task Force estimated that the costs of congestion to industry were £15 billion a year, almost two thirds of which related to waste in London and the South East. Put another way, it was stated that congestion added £10 per week to the average household budget – it costs major commercial transport companies many millions of pounds a year in increased costs and, in turn, these have to be passed on to consumers in the form of higher prices. By 1999, it was estimated that congestion costs had increased to £20 billion a year, an increase of one-third in just ten years.

Congestion is not new! In Ancient Rome, for example, chariots were prohibited from using the streets between daylight and dusk owing to serious congestion problems. More recently, in Victorian times most towns and cities were heavily congested as they struggled to cope with horse-drawn traffic, tramcars and pedestrians fighting to use the narrow streets which were totally unsuitable for the new transport demands being placed upon them.

What is new, though, is the *scale* of the problem. Congestion, in urban areas and on motorways, is now an accepted part of the day-to-day problems of getting around. Moreover, it affects all modes of transport, not just road, although road congestion attracts most attention. With increasing vehicle ownership levels in particular, the demand for transport has outstripped the changes in the supply.

Congestion has one definite outcome – delays! Too much traffic chasing too little road space results in traffic speeds falling to as low as 10 miles/hour (15 km/h) in most cities. This is below our expectations both as drivers and users of public transport. Moreover, the air is thick with poisonous fumes; for motorists and most public transport users, simple journeys are fraught with frustration and stress. Road rage and gridlock are part of the complex problem of congestion.

The costs of traffic congestion

Traffic congestion is a good example of **market failure**; social efficiency is not achieved for the reasons stated above. Consequently, the actions of road users affect people other than themselves, so causing side effects or externalities.

The externalities caused by congestion are invariably *negative*; that is, the marginal social benefit of using cars is less than the marginal private benefit. This is illustrated in Figure 13, in which DD is the demand curve for travel. The vehicle miles demanded will be Q_1 when the price to motorists is P_1 (this is the cost of using the vehicle, per mile). The social optimum is at E_1, where price = marginal social benefit. There is over-consumption of $Q_1 - Q_2$.

The additional monetary costs of congestion can be illustrated by a simple example. Suppose 1000 vehicles are travelling along a congested road at 10 mph. The cost per vehicle of this journey is £2. If a further vehicle uses the road, the speed of traffic would fall below 10 mph and the cost per vehicle would increase slightly, say to £2.01. The private cost to the new driver is £2.01, the same as to all other drivers. The external cost imposed on other drivers by this particular driver, though, is substantial (1000 × 1p = £10). The marginal social cost, therefore, of just one vehicle adding to the traffic flow on a congested road is £12.01. It is relatively easy to comprehend why traffic congestion is so wasteful and so expensive when this principle is applied to a heavily congested road network.

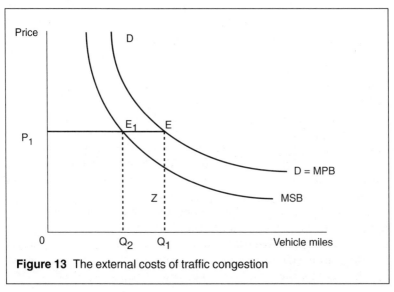

Figure 13 The external costs of traffic congestion

Measurement of the costs of congestion in practice is a complex calculation and includes:

- additional value of time costs to motorists, particularly for work journeys
- increased fuel and other running costs
- reduced vehicle productivity, particularly for goods vehicles
- additional costs to users and operators of public transport services.

An even more complex estimate of the costs of congestion would be if the cost of other negative externalities (arising from exhaust fumes for example) were included.

Policy approaches for relieving congestion

Over the years many approaches have been put forward for dealing with the problem of traffic congestion in cities. Most of these have been planning or engineering solutions, which have little to do with economics and involve the following:

- *Making better use of the road network* – this is a typical approach put forward by traffic engineers and can involve controlling parking on busy roads, creating urban clearways and bus lanes, improving road junctions and park-and-ride schemes.
- *Building more roads* – a natural solution in many respects and one that has been persistently practised in many towns and cities. Realistically, infrastructure development is necessary, but the problem is that our ability to construct, fund and accept new road schemes, particularly in urban areas, is below what is necessary to enhance the flow of traffic. There is also the additional problem that when new roads are built, this tends in itself to generate an increase in demand.
- *Improving public transport* – this is a logical approach that has been pursued with much more vigour in the rest of Europe, where many cities have integrated efficient passenger transport systems which receive substantial subsidies. With the exception of a few projects such as the Tyne and Wear Metro and the more recent new tramway developments in Manchester, Sheffield and elsewhere, this approach has not been favoured by the UK central government since 1979, even though local support may have been extensive.
- *Increasing the cost of urban travel to motorists* through a variety of existing and proposed fiscal measures (see Figure 14). Increased fuel costs, parking charges and so on are one approach; another distinct possibility for the future is road pricing, which is discussed below.

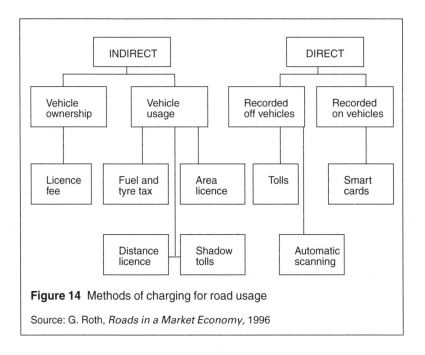

Figure 14 Methods of charging for road usage

Source: G. Roth, *Roads in a Market Economy,* 1996

The merits of road pricing

The basic principle of **road pricing** *is that users should pay the costs they impose on others.*

Road pricing is seen by many economists as the only realistic solution to the problem of urban road congestion. The basic principle stated above makes it different from all other proposed approaches. It is also the only one which is economically efficient. Moreover, road pricing ensures that the prices charged for transport services are more or less in line with their costs – as a result, the market mechanism can allocate traffic efficiently to different modes of transport.

Road pricing should not be considered in isolation – it should be seen as part of a set of measures including those of traffic management and public transport improvement outlined above. It must also be recognised that road pricing is potentially a very contentious issue. A sure way for a government to lose an election is to say that it is introducing road pricing! Realistically, therefore, road pricing is likely to be introduced on a limited basis only – such as the controversial scheme for Cambridge announced in 1991 but then scrapped for political rather than transport expediency.

Figure 15 shows the basic principles behind road pricing. Assuming that road space is in unlimited supply and that it is provided free to

No-go Britain: 1996 indicators

Britain's roads, home to Europe's heaviest traffic, will become even more clogged in 1996. Traffic will grow by around 4 per cent, but the country's road system will expand not at all. There will be around 22m cars on British roads next year; in 2000 there will be at least 25m. The cost of the resulting jam to the economy (and tempers) will be huge.

Although many of Britain's motorways have room for more traffic, congestion will concentrate in Britain's economic heartlands, areas where traffic jams already cost £15 billion ($23 billion) a year. Europe's busiest motorway, the London orbital M25, serves two of the world's biggest airports. If passengers cannot reach Heathrow, the planes will head elsewhere in Europe.

New roads might solve the problem. But thanks to Britain's vocal anti-car lobby (and collapsing government funding) very few will be built. Even plans to complete a small but vital link from the south coast to the Midlands, bypassing the market town of Newbury, have been delayed repeatedly. Britain's last major motorway has already opened. Rail, too, could soak up the excess, but in the throes of privatisation it is shedding, not gaining, traffic.

Some claim electronic traffic-management is the answer. A trial scheme near London lowers speed limits at peak times; it will probably reach most urban motorways by 2000. 'Intelligent' cars may also help. On-board radar systems will allow drivers to bunch together; satellite navigation systems will help them avoid traffic jams. Government ministers even enthuse about toll roads, despite the likely political cost. But none of these systems will increase road capacity on key routes fast enough. Expect to see some spectacular traffic jams in the coming years.

Source: *The World in 1996,* © Economist Publications, 1996

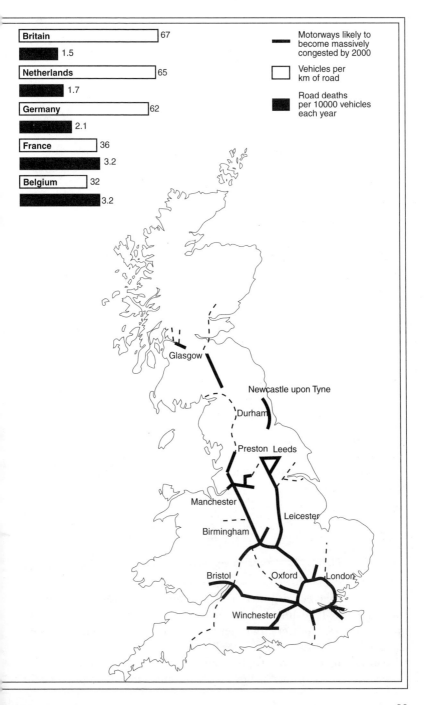

Britain 67
1.5

Netherlands 65
1.7

Germany 62
2.1

France 36
3.2

Belgium 32
3.2

Motorways likely to become massively congested by 2000

Vehicles per km of road

Road deaths per 10000 vehicles each year

Glasgow

Newcastle upon Tyne

Durham

Preston Leeds

Manchester

Leicester

Birmingham

Bristol   Oxford   London

Winchester

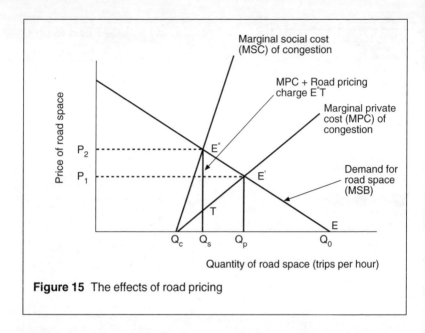

Figure 15 The effects of road pricing

users, consumers will demand Q_0 at zero price. This is the basic market equilibrium. The assumption of unlimited supply is unrealistic – any road has a capacity by definition, which can be shown at Q_c on the diagram. The marginal private cost curve, which shows the supply of road space for users, can be drawn upwards from this point. Equilibrium now is at E', where MPC = MSB; that is, motorists are paying the private costs of using their vehicles. This is *not* the socially optimum point, as road users impose externalities on all other road users, as the earlier numerical example indicated. Hence, the social costs of congestion exceed the private costs – the MSC curve is above that of the MPC. If all of these costs were taken into account, the social optimum would be E'', where the volume of demand is less and the price paid by road users is higher than the market determined equilibrium.

The theory behind road pricing is that the road tax charged to users should equal the cost of the congestion caused. It can be shown on Figure 14 by the magnitude $E''T$. The additional charge for the use of road space will result in a fall in demand from Q_p to Q_s and an increase in price to users. In other words, the loss of welfare has been removed, so that now MSC = MSB at E''.

Road pricing is a particularly good example of an economist's solution which is fine in theory but subject to much debate in practice. In

Road pricing: a radical approach

The political problem that we face lies simply in this: that roads have no asset value, so it cannot seem equitable to charge for their use. And the answer that we give must be as radical as the objections that we face.

This has been accepted by most, if not all, of the authors who have worked on the problem since Professor Smeed made the first serious attempt to face it. But more recently the idea of 'road pricing' has become politically respectable, and it is here that economists must make a stand, and ensure that the principles involved are not obscured ... pricing is to be seen as the sensible way of dealing with the problem of a scarce resource which currently is inefficiently used. It may be the 'least worst' solution, but, if it is to lead to greater efficiency, then its true purpose must be understood.

For misunderstandings already proliferate. The misleading notion that pricing is about deterrence is not far from the surface in the government's recent White Paper. There could be no worse assumption, and it is but a short step to the anti-car prejudice, that is itself as dangerously irrational as most other single-issue movements ... road pricing is just what the words mean; not a tax, not a constraint upon liberty, but a realistic application of economic theory to a serious problem, not easily to be solved in any other way.

This does not mean that road pricing is necessarily an easy solution itself. It were well if it could be developed in the context of a 'Roadtrack' authority, such as Professor Newbery has advocated, so as to form part of a rational policy for the provision and maintenance of roads in general. There is a clear need, as Professor Day argues, for the contemporaneous development of new and improved roads. Mere deterrence, combined with what Professor Foster has called an 'atavistic' approach to road building, will not contribute to economic efficiency. Thirty-five years after Professor Smeed established the principles and practice of road pricing – neither of which has changed significantly in the interim – there is a real danger that the principles will be lost in a fog of political misconceptions.

What is perhaps the *pons asinorum* for all who debate the practical aspects of road pricing is the desired effect that people will use public transport in place of the private car. The freight transport and distribution industry will adapt to pricing because it is already highly competitive and firms are well aware of their marginal costs. The motorist cannot be expected to respond in quite such an objective way. To start with, labour is not a significant part of the motorist's costs, while the typical car owner undoubtedly perceives the costs as far lower than in fact they are. (For most people, a full tank of petrol, once paid for, is seen as a fixed cost until it has to be filled up again, while depreciation is an irrelevant concept.) Contrary to the beliefs of the politically correct, the attraction of the car is far from the emotional prejudice that is commonly supposed. For a wide range of purposes, the car is preferable to public transport on any scale of generalised cost.

If road pricing, then, could be set so as to reflect the actual scarcity value of sections of road at various times and places (pricing that would need to be set heuristically, until a free flow of traffic is attained), congestion would, by definition, have disappeared. At that stage, too, the bus industry would have been able to improve the quality of its product so as to offer an acceptable alternative for those for whom the road price was too high. (The ability of trains and trams to do this is limited by their high investment costs, and by the lack of available land for expansion.) The problem that has to be addressed is the process of moving from present congestion to future efficiency.

Source: Adapted from John Hibbs, *Economic Affairs,* Vol. 18 No. 4
Institute of Economic Affairs, December 1998

Combating congestion –
Singapore has done it!

Singapore has developed a unique approach for dealing with its problems of traffic congestion. This policy, which dates back to the early 1970s, has been implemented by an authoritarian government, determined to:

- limit the use of cars and lorries
- provide an effective mass rapid transit system.

The policy of *restricting car use* is multi-dimensional and involves:

- payment of a massive *first registration fee* on new vehicles, equivalent to around the purchase price for an average family car; considerably higher for company-owned and large engined vehicles
- a *City Area licence charge* payable annually for all private vehicles travelling into central Singapore during the morning peak with fewer than four occupants
- *electronic road pricing* charged on all vehicles used in the central city zone – this charge is made automatically using smart card in-vehicle technology
- a *high rate of taxation* on fuel and an annual vehicle registration fee and road tax; a weekend only discount on the annual registration charge is available; high central area parking charges

Singapore has used the money from the taxation of private cars to fund a highly effective *MRT system.* This is heavily used for work purposes and other trips into the central area. Fares are relatively cheap due to

---

recent years, advanced technology has made it easier to work out the actual cost of congestion caused by the individual motorist (see the case of Singapore).

Road pricing does have certain important *advantages*:

- It is a market-based solution to the problem of congestion.
- It is the only solution to congestion that is likely to result in a fall in traffic and an increase in vehicle speeds.
- Revenue from road pricing could be used to fund improvements in public transport.

Its critics point to certain *disadvantages*, namely:

- It is socially divisive in so far as all road users will pay the same level of charge at a particular time, irrespective of their incomes. Under

No room, no room

Singapore invented it. Norway copied it. Stockholm spent 20 years and $1 billion before thinking again. Hong Kong retreated at the last moment in the face of a popular revolt. Politicians are terrified of road pricing. How can you get people to pay for something that has always been free? ...

The motives for charging vary. Many countries, notably Spain, France, Italy and Japan, and several American states have long collected tolls as a way of financing the building of new motorways. In New Zealand, road users pay directly for roads through vehicle-licence fees, a levy on gasoline and weight-distance charges for heavy goods vehicles. The latest automated tolling equipment, which deducts charges from electronically tagged vehicles, is being installed in more than 20 countries around the world. The tags are linked to in-car meters which can be loaded either with a pre-set credit or used to log travel for billing later. Charging, aimed at deterring excess traffic from entering cities, is more controversial but is gaining acceptance...

In Europe, road-pricing schemes have been success-fully operated for more than five years in Trondheim, Bergen and Oslo. Trondheim, Norway's third-largest city, desperately needed a ring-road to stop huge flows of traf-fic coming through the centre of town. After much debate, the local council hit upon the idea of charging for access to the city centre, by putting up a ring of 12 toll stations, and using the revenues to pay for the construction of the new road. A high tariff applies from 6am till 10am, a lower one from then till 5pm. After that, travel is free until next morning. There is also a discount for cars with an elec-tronic tag which allows them to go through tolls without stopping, thereby reducing the congestion caused by toll queues...

The Netherlands has a more ambitious plan to introduce road pricing, covering the densely populated Randstad area of the four main towns, Amsterdam, Rotterdam, Utrecht and the Hague. It is due to come into effect in 2001. Cars will have to carry a smart card containing cash credits that can also be used for other transactions. The charge for driving into each of the four cities will be set high, at about 15 ecus ($17), between 6am and 10am, but the price will fall to 3 ecus at other times. Non-payers will be caught on video cameras and sent a bill by the tax office, using the registration details culled from the number plate... There is still some debate about whether the proceeds should be returned to the public in lower taxes or whether they should all be spent on public transport.

In France ... last August, the environment minister was scorched by the press when pollution in cities such as Paris, Lyons and Strasbourg rose to the so-called third level, at which it is generally considered dangerous to many frail people and damaging to the lungs of the population at large. By September, when fine weather produced more smog, the government banned cars from entering Paris on alternate days, according to whether they had odd- or even-numbered licence plates, and made public transport free.

Britain and Germany are much less advanced, but both have conducted trials of urban and motorway road pricing. Field trials in Leicester and Stuttgart have sought to establish how high charges must be before motorists are persuaded to leave their car behind and switch to other forms of transport...

From now on politics, not technology, will dictate the pace of change... As more and more charging schemes are implemented and the benefits of less congested, unpolluted roads are felt, attitudes will change. In 20 years' time, people will look back and wonder why they were ever prepared to put up with the pollution, noise and paralysis of today's cities.

Source: Abridged from *The Economist*, 6–12 December 1997

If you think it's bad in Britain ... it is far, far worse in Bangkok!

For the citizens of Bangkok, one of Asia's megacities, traffic congestion impinges upon all aspects of life – environmental quality, human health, quality of life, lifestyle, stress levels and so on are directly affected by the city's phenomenal transport problem. The population of Bangkok is increasing at around 2 per cent a year and has doubled in the last 25 years. As in all parts of Asia, vehicle ownership levels are increasing at a substantial rate, a consequence of economic advancement. In Bangkok alone it is estimated that:

- 800 new vehicles a day are fighting to use the road network.
- Residents spend an average of 44 working days a year stuck in traffic.
- Lost production due to congestion amounts to 10 per cent of Thailand's GNP.
- Peak period vehicle speeds of 6 km are the norm.

The major economic and health impacts are shown below.

Economic impacts
- $9.6 billion per year lost output, and $1.6 billion per year energy wasted by vehicles stuck in traffic jams
- Millions of dollars of additional health costs

Health impacts
- CO_2 and particulate emissions 18 times greater than WHO maximum guidelines
- 42 per cent of traffic police have a respiratory disease
- 1 million people per year suffer from respiratory diseases linked to air pollution
- Bangkok's rate of lung cancer is three times Thailand's average
- Lead levels in children's' blood is three times WHO maximum guidelines
- Nervous strain and stress owing to traffic congestion

Source: Adapted from P. du Pont and K. Egan, *World Transport Policy & Practice,* Vol. 3, No. 1, 1997

certain circumstances, it could actually be progressive, although this argument is seldom recognized.
- There are genuine problems of estimating the external costs of traffic congestion and establishing these in relation to road pricing charges.
- The technology, although much advanced in recent years, is relatively unproved and could be subject to abuse and evasion.

- The level of charge must be carefully fixed in relation to the price elasticity of demand for travel if congestion levels are to be reduced.

Road pricing in practice

The practical application of road pricing is best seen in Singapore, where a city Area Licensing Scheme has been in operation for over 20 years. Initially, this was a very crude system whereby vehicles entering the city centre between 7.30 a.m. and 9.30 a.m. had to pay an area licence charge. The outcome was an immediate reduction in cars travelling during the peak period and a significant increase in traffic speed. An evening peak charge was introduced later, followed by a scheme whereby anyone purchasing a new car has to be in possession of a COE before they can purchase a vehicle. The cost of the COE is very high and determined by market prices – a figure of $60 000 (£20 000) was the typical cost of a COE for a medium sized car in early 1995!

Singapore is an unusual, and in some respects unique, case. Road pricing and the COE system are just a part of a much more comprehensive set of transport policies seeking to reduce congestion in the city. It also leads the world when it comes to direct charging for congestion. The cities of Oslo and Bergen in Norway have cordon charges which apply for large periods of the day, and in Hong Kong a pilot scheme involving the use of electronic number plates has been tried out.

Within the UK, the administrative and legislative framework is now in place for road pricing schemes to be developed and implemented by local authorities over a ten-year period from 2000. The New Deal White Paper (see Chapter 7) recognized the role that could be played through deliberate intervention in the prices charged for transport. This theme was reinforced in the 'Breaking the logjam' consultation document which clearly encouraged local authorities to:

- produce local transport plans which could include provision for road user charges (as road pricing now tends to be called) and levies on workplace parking
- plan transport improvements such as new tram systems from hypothecated revenue from user charging schemes
- see the possibilities of the above as a means of solving local congestion problems.

Just where such schemes will be introduced in the UK outside London is difficult to assess. A pilot project was carried out in Leicester (see data response question); Leeds, Manchester, Bristol and Birmingham have all indicated that they are considering introducing road pricing over the next few years as part of their local transport plans. Beyond these places and a few historic towns, user charging will not be pursued unless local plans see it as a positive means for dealing with the problem of congestion.

The case in London is different. The Mayor, Ken Livingstone, is firmly committed to introducing a charging system by 2002 or 2003 (see box). The revenue from such a scheme would, in turn, provide funding for major public transport improvements. Unlike in other cities, the Mayor of London has the powers to be able to do this and interestingly, most people who live or work in London actually recognize that overall, charging will provide net benefits in the form of less

Drivers face £5-a-day fee to enter London

ANDY McSMITH

Drivers in central London will be charged £5 a day, or £15 a day for a lorry, in an experiment to reduce traffic jams and pollution, and raise about £200 million for public transport.

Charges are likely to apply between 7am and 7pm every working day and would be enforced by digital cameras able to read vehicle registration marks.

Drivers would pay the charge on the day, or in advance through garages, newsagents and shops, by post, or telephone, or the internet. Evaders would be fined £100.

Charges would apply to all vehicles except buses, black cabs, police cars, fire engines, ambulances and vehicles with disabled drivers. Minicabs might be exempt.

The scheme would apply in the central part of London bounded by the inner ring road which runs alongside Hyde Park, south to Elephant and Castle, east to Tower Bridge and north to Euston station.

Congestion charges were an issue on which Ken Livingstone, the London mayor, fought his campaign. He has the power to introduce them without the Government's approval.

Yesterday he set out his 'early thinking' to test the views of about 300 'key traffic stakeholders'. The public will be asked their views later.

The charges, expected to be introduced late in 2002 or early the following year, are predicted to cut traffic by about 12 per cent, with non-payers running an 80 per cent chance of being caught.

An estimated one million people work in central London and about one in seven commutes by car. At peak times more than 50,000 vehicles an hour enter the city centre.

Loud complaints are expected, particularly from residents inside the congestion charge zone. They will not be charged the full £5 a day, but will have to pay an annual fee, probably £100.

Source: *Daily Telegraph,* 29 July 2000

road congestion and better public transport services. This degree of support is unusual.

Apart from these examples, the practical problems of introducing road pricing have so far deterred other cities looking for a solution to their congestion problems. It remains to be seen whether the growing consensus amongst transport economists in favour of road pricing will actually be matched by its practical implementation.

What is now clear is that economists, transport planners, politicians and even motorists are increasingly moving away from Mrs Thatcher's vision of 'the great car economy'. The costs of congestion are now so great that they cannot be ignored. As *The Economist* powerfully states, road pricing tomorrow is the only solution to jam today – the ball is now firmly in the politicians' court.

KEY WORDS

Congestion   Road pricing
Market failure

Further reading

Anderton, A., Unit 62 in *Economics*, 3rd edn, Causeway Press, 2000.

Burningham, D., and Davies, J., Chapters 4 and 5 in *Green Economics*, 2nd edn, Heinemann, 1999.

Munday, S., Chapter 8 in *Markets and Market Failure*, Heinemann, 2000.

Sloman, J., Chapter 12 in *Economics*, 4th edn, Pearson Education, 2000.

Useful website

UK Environment Protection Agency: www.environment-agency.gov.uk

Essay topics

1. The most recent estimate (in 1998) of the costs of traffic congestion in the UK was put at £19 billion per year, a 25 per cent increase since 1989.

    (a) Explain the basis on which economists estimate the costs of traffic congestion.   [10 marks]

    (b) Discuss how the costs of traffic congestion affect road transport companies, manufacturers and the economy as a whole.
                                                                  [10 marks]

[OCR, March 2000]

2. (a) Discuss the arguments for and against the introduction of road pricing in a congested city such as London. [8 marks]

   (b) Why might these arguments not necessarily apply to all congested cities? [12 marks]

Data response question

This task is from an OCR examination paper in November 2000. Read the extract and study the data on toll charges, then answer the questions that follow.

The Leicester Road Pricing trial

For many years, economists have maintained that road pricing is the only realistic means available for reducing the problem of traffic congestion in the UK's towns and cities. They have argued that if the daily toll or charge for entry into city centres is set at a high enough rate, there is a 'breaking point' at which motorists will abandon their cars and use other modes of transport. Until the recent experimental trial in Leicester, there has been no clear evidence as to how much the toll must be for this to happen. The underlying principles are a particular application of the concept of price elasticity of demand.

In the Leicester trial, 60 volunteer motorists took part in a six month trial scheme whereby they were given 'smart cards' with a spending limit of £120 per month and told that they could keep any money saved using alternative modes of transport such as buses, bicycles or walking. Various levels of charges were made for their daily commuting journeys into Leicester for varying periods of time between August 1997 and March 1998. Table A shows the measured effects of these variations on this group of motorists.

Alongside this experiment, from August 1997, a new park and ride shuttle bus service and priority lanes were set up. As a consequence, it was quicker for motorists to travel into Leicester using park and ride than by car. If the trial becomes reality, the city's planners intend to hypothecate the revenue from toll charges into a new rapid transit system, better bus services and other measures designed to provide real choice for Leicester's long-suffering commuters.

Table A How the toll charges affected choice of transport

Time period operated 1997/98	Toll charge (£ per day)	% Commuting by Car	Park & Ride	Other
August	£1.50	80	15	5
Sept–Nov	£3.00	80	15	5
December	£6.00	50	35	15
Jan–Feb	£4.00	75	20	5
March	£5.00	65	30	5

1. Briefly explain what is meant by 'road pricing'. [4 marks]
2. Use the information provided in Table A to:
   (a) Explain how the price elasticity of demand for travel into Leicester by car varies with the level of toll charged. [4 marks]
   (b) Suggest what level of toll might be charged for there to be a significant reduction in car commuting traffic into Leicester. Justify your answer. [3 marks]
3. Explain the likely reasons why 'the city planners intend to hypothecate the revenue from toll charges into a new rapid transit system'. [3 marks]
4. Comment upon why road pricing may *not* be acceptable to all vehicle users wishing to travel into the centre of Leicester. [6 marks]

Chapter Seven
Transport policy for the twenty-first century

'The White Paper reflects the Government's commitment to giving transport the highest possible priority. We now look to others – companies, individuals, employees and local authorities – to join us in shaping a new future for sustainable transport in the UK.' John Prescott MP, Foreword to New Deal White Paper, 1998

The problem we face

The transport revolution of the past 50 years has brought considerable advantages in terms of personal mobility and choice to the ever-increasing proportion of the population able to take advantage of it. There have simultaneously been benefits to business and those involved in the transport of freight. Let us not forget this. As the twenty-first century unfolds though, the problems brought by this revolution are clear for all to see. Specifically:

- Traffic congestion in major towns and cities and in London is getting worse.
- Traffic volumes on most motorways are reaching the point of capacity saturation (see Figure 16).
- User expectations are no longer being met, journey times are more unpredictable and there is a tremendous wastage of human and business resources.
- The opportunities gained by the railways as a consequence of privatization are in danger of not being fully realized.
- There are worrying concerns about the impact of atmospheric pollution, noise and intrusion on the lives and well-being of millions of people.
- Real choice is being denied for groups in the community such as the elderly, non-car owners and those living in rural areas.

And if this state of affairs was not worrying enough, no comfort can be derived from the most recent road traffic forecasts which predict a rise in private car traffic levels of 36–57 per cent by 2020 (see Figure 17). Assuming no major changes in transport policy, a zero increase in bus use is also being forecast. In short, it seems a miserable prospect for 17-year-olds who have just passed their driving tests!

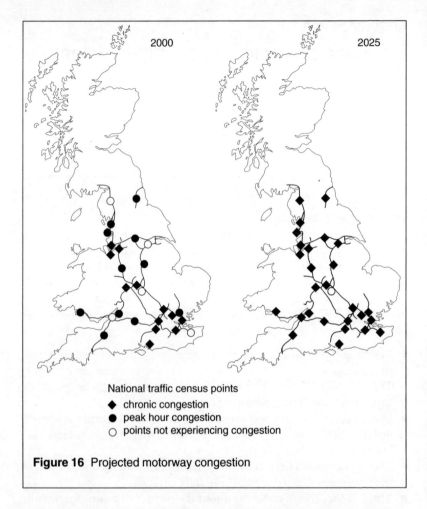

National traffic census points
- ◆ chronic congestion
- ● peak hour congestion
- ○ points not experiencing congestion

Figure 16 Projected motorway congestion

To economists, the concern is that a massive misallocation of resources has occurred and that, as Figure 18 indicates, the gap between forecast demand and supply is widening and will continue to diverge over the next few years. It is against this background that the government has sought to re-position its transport policy in order to meet the needs of people and industry in the twenty-first century.

The new transport policy

The principal objective of transport policy remains unchanged and is one of 'achieving an efficient allocation of resources in transport'. In this respect, the new transport policy is no different to that which has

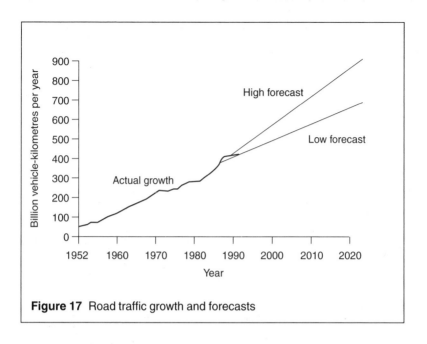

Figure 17 Road traffic growth and forecasts

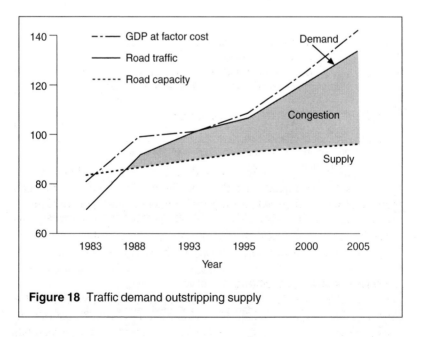

Figure 18 Traffic demand outstripping supply

operated since the nationalization of transport in 1947. What is different though are the additional requirements that:

- the quality, availability and price of transport should be such that individuals and businesses should be able to fulfil their derived demands for transport services
- transport should not have further negative effects upon the quality of life

---

Sustainable distribution

Road freight transport and distribution have an important role in delivering goods and services to enable the economy to operate effectively and to provide for the daily needs of industry and commerce. The industry has made important efficiency gains over the last twenty years – 15 per cent fewer vehicles in 2001 are carrying a greater volume of traffic than in 1984. There is though a very real need to make distribution even more sustainable. This was the purpose of a Government consultation document published in March 1999.

Distribution can and must become more sustainable through a variety of measures including:

- switching even more goods from road to rail transport
- reducing the amount of empty running by goods vehicles – at present, about one third of all vehicle mileage is by vehicles carrying no load. Load factors can also be improved
- encouraging firms to co-operate in their use of goods vehicles. Relevant measures include shared-user distribution whereby companies, sometimes competitors, join together for their distribution requirements for some customers
- using better fuel management, vehicle routing and tracking systems to cut out unnecessary waste
- a reduction in the amount of avoidable waste materials used in the distribution function. With packaging especially, there are many opportunities to recycle used material or cut back on the use of materials made from non-renewable resources
- changes to the way in which vehicles are taxed to make it more expensive to operate those which are not very environmentally acceptable. This a very important principle of current government policy.

More far-reaching proposals could make the distribution function even more sustainable than at present. In particular these involve the more extensive use of local sourcing, so cutting back of vehicle mileage. Local 'just in time' systems have much to commend from a sustainability standpoint - Japanese motor assembly plants in the UK have been very efficient in this respect.

- transport should contribute fully to the New Economy of the twenty-first century, yet at the same time promote the longer-term objective of **sustainability**
- **real choice** should be provided for users of transport.

Integration has again come to the fore and has an important role to play in the new transport policy. In principle, an integrated transport policy is one which covers all modes of transport, for passengers and for freight. In other words, it is an all-embracing policy which clearly sets out the relationship between road, rail, air and sea transport. It is though an ideal which has not yet been achieved in the UK, specifically because of the problem of establishing the competitive relationship between road and rail transport. As analysed in Chapter 5, through deregulation and privatization this relationship is becoming a little clearer, but there is still a long way to go.

Notwithstanding, in August 1997, the Labour government made its policy intentions clear in an important consultation document called *Developing an Integrated Transport Policy*. This document stressed the government's intention to carry out a fundamental review of transport policy, particularly for public transport, where it saw most opportunity to develop integration. Significantly also, there was a strong commitment to doing this within the context of an environmentally **sustainable transport** system, entirely consistent with the published views of the Royal Commission on Environmental Pollution (see box on page 106). Let us now look at integration and sustainability in transport in more detail.

One of the most common complaints from users of public transport is that services are seemingly unco-ordinated, unstructured and not linked together. This can apply to:

- links between particular rail services or bus services
- links between the private car and all forms of public transport
- links between road and rail-freight transport and distribution terminals.

The deregulation of local bus services and the setting up of privatized, sometimes rival, train operating companies has often promoted disintegration (see Chapter 5). The government's intention is to reverse this trend by achieving more integration through:

- easier and better connections for bus and rail users
- better information systems (e.g. a national bus and rail enquiry system)
- safer and more conveniently located interchanges
- improved ticketing systems, allowing passengers to buy one com-

Twentieth Report of the Royal Commission on Environmental Pollution: main points

- *Fuel consumption of cars must be reduced*
  In particular, higher taxes should be introduced on cars with big engines, multi-purpose vehicles and 4 x 4 vehicles such as the 3.5-litre engine Shogun and Vauxhall Monterey.

- *Heavy lorries using motorways should be required to have a permit*
  Similar to the vignette system introduced in some other EU countries; designed to help UK and especially non-UK hauliers pay towards the additional wear and tear caused by their vehicles; likely to induce more freight to use rail.

- *Tighter EU limits on emissions from new vehicles*
  Limits have now come into effect and will be followed by even tighter limits by 2005.

- *Raise fuel prices by more than 6 per cent per year*
  Part of an additional strategy to raise real fuel prices; minor concessions for low-sulphur diesel and other less polluting fuels. Abolish leaded petrol.

- *Local councils should be able to charge for road use*
  Very clear support for selective road pricing schemes (see Chapter 6); local authorities should also be encouraged to charge for private non-residential parking.

- *Improved provision of access into towns and cities for cyclists and buses*
  Urban cycleways and bus lanes should be extended, with particular priorities given at road junctions.

- *Greater integration of transport and land use planning*
  Urban design and transport planning should not be focused on car dependence; out-of-town controls on new shopping and commercial developments should remain.

bined ticket covering more than one mode of transport (e.g. similar to those being promoted in most conurbations by the passenger transport executives)
- purpose-built freight interchanges (e.g. the Daventry International Freight Terminal) and transhipment points close to main cities.

Some aspects of this policy have already occurred; others will be implemented over the next few years. Through improved integration, public transport and rail freight become more attractive – the outcome is more sustainable than road-only transport.

The principle of sustainability is relatively new and is one which is being applied to many areas of economic activity, transport included. It involves the application of a deliberate approach whereby the needs of the present are met without compromising the ability of future generations to meet their own needs. In simple terms, it means that transport policy today must be focused, for the reasons described earlier in this chapter, to ensure that in 25–30 years' time there is a transport network which provides for the needs of passenger and freight users.

There is overwhelming evidence that future estimates of resource consumption, CO_2 emissions, vehicle numbers and the distances they travel are not sustainable. Over the past 30 years or so, motor vehicle traffic growth has continued to outstrip GDP growth. With no change in transport policy this can be expected to continue. Transport's share of CO_2 emissions in the UK has also increased as traffic levels have increased. Neither is there enough physical space or government expenditure to meet forecast demand. The wider implications, in terms of climatic change, are worrying and cannot be ignored by those who have a responsibility to future generations. Additionally, the social effects of this so-called '**overshoot**' are a cause for concern.

The problems above are not unique to the UK. The question of CO_2 emissions, global warming and climatic change has concerned world political leaders since 1988, when at the Rio Summit targets were set for reducing emissions of greenhouse gases. Transport is a major contributor to CO_2 emissions in the UK – it is, though, not the only contributor. In 1997, the UK government made the bold statement that it would seek to reduce CO_2 emissions by a higher rate than had previously been targeted. If this is to be achieved, there is little argument that it will need to be done through a much more sustainable national transport policy.

'A New Deal for Transport – Better for Everyone'

The principles of integration and sustainability are the twin pillars of this White Paper which was presented to Parliament in July 1998. Its

'A New Deal for Transport': main points

For car drivers

- Increased taxes of £1 billion by 2005. These include city centre access charges, workplace parking levies and charges to enter popular countryside areas.
- Pilot motorway charging schemes.
- **Hypothecation** of additional taxes to public transport improvement. This is the first time that this principle has been agreed by government.

For public transport

- £300 million new investment in light rail transit especially.
- Improved interchange facilities.
- More bus priority schemes.
- A national information system.
- Quality partnerships.
- National concessionary fares scheme.

For railways

- A new Strategic Rail Authority.
- £300 million new investment to add to that from private sector.
- Likely tax relief for regular travellers.

For freight transport

- More incentives to switch from road to rail.
- Encourage use of vehicles with six axles.
- Quality partnerships.

For pedestrians and cyclists

- More cycle lanes in towns and cities.
- Experimental schemes to encourage children to walk or cycle to school.
- More 'lollipop' persons with greater powers.
- Campaigners to get motorists to walk for short trips.

main details are shown in the boxed item. Overall, it provided a major boost for public transport, the bus especially, and put forward various proposals to encourage the greater use of those modes of transport which are most sustainable.

What was also new were the various new structures which were to be set up in order to meet the above objectives. These included:

- a Strategic Rail Authority (see Chapter 5)
- a Commission on Integrated Transport which was given the task of promoting better integration in passenger and freight transport
- local Quality Partnerships for bus and freight transport whereby local government and transport users and providers could meet to tackle various local problems
- legislation to give local authorities new powers to be able to charge tolls for access into major towns and cities.

Viewed overall, it is a radical change of direction of national transport policy. It is also revolutionary as for the most part, it is merely seeking to put into place what most long-suffering transport users know to be the correct policy, which is one of providing a better deal, with more real choice, for all transport users.

Ten-year transport plan to 2010

The most controversial aspect of the New Deal White Paper, with the benefit of hindsight, was its clear statement that 'The days of predict and provide are over – we will give top priority to improving the main-

---

Ten-year transport plan to 2010

Roads
- Major widening schemes for 360 miles of motorways and trunk roads
- 100 new by-passes
- Many local road improvements

Rail
- Huge capital injection from public and private sector to upgrade West Coast, East Coast and Great Western Main Lines
- Easing of strategic network bottlenecks in West Midlands and Manchester areas
- New East–West link for London and increase in trans-Pennine capacity
- Upgrade of links to deep-sea container ports

Trams and buses
- New networks for Leeds, Portsmouth, Bristol and Merseyside; extensions in Birmingham and Manchester

---

tenance and management of existing roads before building new ones'. In short, no more new major road schemes (see also Chapter 4).

It was therefore something of a surprise when in July 2000 the government published an important new ten-year transport plan which sought to reduce road congestion by building more new roads. An estimated £124 billion was expected to be allocated in the plan – over one-third of which was to be spent on the road network. It could be argued with some justification that the government had finally abandoned all hope of reducing and reversing the rate of growth of road traffic.

The plan also contained important proposals for increased investment in the rail network, for passengers and freight, and for major improvements to public transport in a selected number of cities which was much more in line with the strategies contained in the New Deal White Paper. The boxed item shows some of the main points of this important plan.

The price of fuel – making it happen?

The New Deal White Paper contained a very clear statement on the government's attitude towards the price of fuel, namely that increasing fuel duty would continue to be part of the strategy for tackling climatic change brought about by increasing CO_2 emissions. Moreover, the high price of petrol and diesel encourages some drivers to re-consider their mode of transport for certain journeys and provides an incentive to vehicle manufacturers to produce vehicles which are more fuel efficient. It is also firmly stated that the so-called Escalator would remain, resulting in annual fuel duty increases of at least 6 per cent above the rate of inflation, 1 per cent higher than the Conservatives' commitment. In short, the high price of fuel is essential for the objectives of a more sustainable transport policy.

During 1999 and 2000 the retail price of fuel increased by over 30 per cent (see Table 18). The main cause of this increase was not so much due to the Escalator as to the massive increase in world fuel prices largely as a consequence of a cut in the supply of crude oil on to the world market by OPEC producers. As demand was unchecked, basic economic analysis points to the obvious outcome that prices will rise. This rise in fuel prices persisted due to the depreciation of sterling against the US dollar particularly during the summer months of 2000. By October, the world price of crude oil was $36 per barrel, its highest since 1974.

Although the government abandoned the Escalator in the Spring Budget, this did little to stifle the growing revolt over the price of fuel,

Table 18 The price of unleaded petrol in the UK (pence)

Month	Lowest price (per litre)	VAT	Excise duty	Refinery cost price
January 1999	61.9	9.22	43.99	4.8
April 1999	67.9	10.11	47.21	7.3
July 1999	68.9	10.26	47.21	8.4
October 1999	71.9	10.71	47.21	10.9
January 2000	72.9	10.86	47.21	11.6
April 2000	77.9	11.60	48.82	13.7
July 2000	82.9	12.35	48.82	17.6
October 2000	77.9	11.60	48.82	16.4

Source: Petrol Retailers Association

led by farmers and hauliers as well as private motorists. In an unprecedented move, demonstrators blocked oil refineries, forcing many filling stations to close as supplies ran dry. Very quickly there was major dislocation to the supplies of food in the retail supply chain. It was at this point that the protestors withdrew, having made their point very determinedly by bringing the country to its knees. Similar protests had also occurred in France, Germany, Spain and the Netherlands. The government remained adamant that it would not cut fuel duty, stating that any review would have to be for the new round of public sector bidding.

The crisis over the price of fuel has caused a major dilemma for the government:

- On the one hand, it has raised serious doubts over the government's commitment to a more sustainable transport policy. Any decrease in fuel duty would not reduce the demand for travel.
- On the other hand, politically, it has to listen to the arguments put forward by the road lobby, a very powerful force in business and the economy.

The boxed item on page 112 indicates very clearly how opinions are seriously divided on this very controversial, politically sensitive matter.

Porritt accuses Blair over 'failure of leadership'

Tony Blair's chief environmental adviser yesterday attacked the government for its 'failure of leadership' in neglecting to explain why high fuel prices were needed to head off disastrous climatic change.

Jonathon Porritt, chairman of the Sustainable Development Commission, criticised the Prime Minister for not referring to Britain's commitments to tackle climatic change or the dangers that global warming poses to Britain while defending high taxes on fuel since his first attack on the Dump the Pump campaign. Mr Blair's view was that high fuel taxes were necessary to pay for spending on schools and hospitals – no mention was made of Britain's strategy to cut 20 per cent of its CO_2 emissions by 2010. Mr Porritt went on to say that 'any cuts in fuel prices would be the worst thing to happen to the environmental movement in 20 years'.

Source: Adapted from the *Daily Telegraph*, 16 September 2000

FTA calls for a massive cut in diesel duty

The Freight Transport Association (FTA), the major trade association for freight distributors and customers, is calling for a 15p per litre cut on diesel duty. David Green, Director General, stressed that this cut would cost the same as a 3p litre across the board cut on all road fuels. He pointed out that it would place the relative cost of diesel compared to petrol on the same basis as on the continent.

The FTA's view is that the high taxation on diesel has starved the industry of cash it needed to invest in new, cleaner vehicles and that it had actually been counter-productive. Moreover, the high price of diesel was putting many hauliers' businesses at risk as they were just not competitive when compared to others in the rest of the EU. It was also forcing more firms to 'flag out' of the UK and establish operating centres in France and Belgium especially.

Source: Adapted from *Freight*, monthly journal of the Freight Transport Association, October 2000

End of term report?

Many readers will have received school reports that say things like

'tries hard but could do better'
'early promise not yet realised'
'key weaknesses need to be urgently addressed for future success'

In many respects, this assessment could also be made of Labour's transport policy since 1997.

More specifically,

- the use of rail and bus passenger transport has bottomed out and appears to be increasing
- rail is moving much more freight
- government spending and private sector investment in transport are at an all time high
- important new structures are in place.

At the same time,

- road congestion is getting worse
- public confidence in rail transport has decreased
- there has been a clear U-turn on policy towards road building
- political errors of judgement on transport issues have been made

Notwithstanding, the future does appear reasonably hopeful. Introducing selective road user charges holds many of the keys to the future success of an integrated transport policy.

So where does this leave us?

Certain aspects of recent transport policy have cast a shadow over the realization of a more sustainable transport policy. In principle such a policy aims:

- to reduce the rate of growth of future demand for transport
- to reduce the future demand for private car transport and road freight
- to promote the increased use of sustainable modes of transport such as walking, cycling, bus and rail.

Although the New Deal White Paper was broadly seeking to achieve a more sustainable policy, recent events have thrown up considerable confusion as to whether this remains an achievable objective. To some extent it appears that the government has now accepted that car use will continue to increase in the future. The only obstacle to this would be a relatively deep recession.

On the other hand, there are still many aspects of current transport policy that are sustainable such as:

- the renewed emphasis on improving the rail and bus networks
- the determination to switch large volumes of freight traffic from road to rail
- selective user charging schemes for entry into city centres which aim to reduce road traffic flows and congestion
- an increased public awareness of the social benefits of walking or cycling for short trips in town and city centres.

Until meaningful choices are provided, there is every likelihood that road traffic will continue to grow. If choice is not happening, then the stakeholders referred to by Mr Prescott will have failed to make their contribution in shaping a new future for sustainable transport in the UK.

KEY WORDS	
Sustainability	Sustainable transport
Real choice	Overshoot
Integration	Hypothecation

Further reading

Bamford, C., (ed.), Chapter 6 in *Economics for AS*, Cambridge University Press, 2000.

Burningham, D., and Davies, J., Chapters 4 and 7 in *Green Economics*, 2nd edn, Heinemann, 1999.

Griffiths, A., and Wall, S., Chapter 12 in *Applied Economics*, 8th edn, Longman, 1999.

Maunder, P. *et al.*, Chapter 10 in *Economics Explained*, 3rd edn, HarperCollins, 2000.

Useful website

UN Commission on Sustainable Development: www.un.org/esa/sust-dev

Essay topics

1. (a) Explain why a 'sustainable transport policy' is needed in the UK. [10 marks]

   (b) Discuss the contribution that economists can make towards the realization of a more sustainable transport policy for the UK. [10 marks]

   [OCR, March 2000]

2. Discuss the advantages and disadvantages of more expensive fuel from the point of view of:

   (a) private motorists

   (b) the road haulage industry

   (c) the government's transport policy. [20 marks]

Data response question

This task is from an OCR examination paper in March 1999. Read the newspaper extract, then answer the questions that follow.

Driven to distractions

'We should have the highest aims for our transport system' declared the Deputy Prime Minister, John Prescott, yesterday. As an avid enthusiast for Jaguar cars. Mr Prescott has always aimed high where transport is concerned. But yesterday, wearing his ministerial hat as Secretary of State for Environment, Transport and the Regions (no less), he urged us all to leave the car at home and make greater use of public transport. To that end there will, he announced, be a fundamental transport review and eventually an integrated transport policy.

An integrated transport policy has long been the holy grail of environmentalists. It is one of those catchphrases that sounds impressive until somebody asks what it might actually mean. More public transport and fewer cars is the usual answer, and most of us would say amen to that. But hitherto, no one has been able convincingly to explain how, in a society as adverse to tax and keen on cars as ours, such a desirable outcome can be achieved. Yesterday, Mr Prescott merely promised 'a long-term strategy White Paper' for next spring.

Unless we are to get stuck in permanent recession, however, the demand for passenger and freight transport will continue to grow, and to a greater or lesser extent all forms of transport pollute. More use of public tranport might slow or even halt the rise in emissions from cars, buses and lorries, but it is hard to see how they can be cut by anything like the amount Mr Prescott apparently envisages. And while public transport is often the best option for commuting or travel within city centres, for most other journeys the car is likely to remain the most practical choice.

So what can the Government do? It can of course raise taxes on petrol and probably will, although the Conservatives were already doing that. To raise them any faster might simply prove inflationary. It can encourage greater investment in public transport, although if it is to do that it had better drop its abusive and menacing attitude towards the privatised bus and train companies. Gestures can give a lead in a cause like this, but they should be positive rather than negative ones. A better example from the top would be a start. It seems inappropriate, to say the least of it, that the Prime Minister has chartered Concorde to take him to the UN General Assembly's Special Session on the Environment later this month. Then there are all those ministers' and mandarins' cars, 200 at the last count. Whitehall is a small village, and its new masters would get a little more exercise by walking around it. Mr Prescott did his bit by travelling on the Tube en route to his speech yesterday. If he really wants to practise what he preaches, perhaps he should get rid of the Jag altogether.

Source: *Daily Telegraph*, 6 June 1997

1. 'Unless we are to get stuck in permanent recession, however, the demand for passenger and freight transport will continue to grow …' Explain the economic relationship involved in this statement.
   [4 marks]
2. (a) What do economists mean by 'an integrated transport policy'?
   [2 marks]
   (b) State and explain *one* obstacle which may make it difficult to achieve such a policy.
   [4 marks]

3. (a) With the aid of a diagram, analyse the effects of higher petrol taxes on the demand for petrol. [2 marks]
   (b) Briefly explain how higher petrol prices might affect the demand for transport. [2 marks]
4. Discuss what means other than petrol taxes the government might use in order to encourage less use of the private car and greater use of public transport. [6 marks]

Conclusion

'We need to learn to strike a better balance between the various modes of transport and give people a real choice for meeting their transport needs' John Prescott MP, Deputy Prime Minister, 1997

It is very fitting that the final epigraph in this book should be a quotation from the Deputy Prime Minister, whose Department of Transport, Environment and the Regions holds many of the means for dealing with the transport problems and issues raised in this text. Whether this will amount to a properly integrated transport policy, covering all modes of passenger and freight transport, remains to be seen.

In recent years, professional transport economists have made an important contribution to the debate on transport policy. Through this book, it is hoped that students of Economics will have grasped an introductory insight into the economic principles which underpin the transport problems subsumed in the debate. The book does not pretend to have the answer – what it does do is provide an analysis of the likely available options for the government to evaluate if it is to provide an efficient and effective transport network to meet the demands and pressures of the twenty first century.

There is a lot at stake. In order to meet the challenge as well as realise the opportunities available, transport needs highly motivated, well qualified staff at all levels and in all types of transport business. It is hoped that this book may have provided some readers with the foundation for future study and possibly a career in a fascinating industry which is vital for our economic and social well-being.

Index